TONGUE IN CHECK

JOSEPH M. STOWELL

While this book is designed for the reader's personal enjoyment and profit, it is also intended for group study. A Leader's Guide with Victor Multiuse Transparency Masters is available from your local bookstore or from the publisher.

VICTOR BOOKS®

A DIVISION OF SCRIPTURE PRESS PUBLICATIONS INC.
USA CANADA ENGLAND

Seventh printing, 1989

Unless otherwise noted, Scripture quotations are from the *Holy Bible, New International Version*, © 1973, 1978, 1984, International Bible Society. Used by permission of Zondervan Bible Publishers. Other quotations are from the *King James Version* (KJV) and the *New American Standard Bible* (NASB), © the Lockman Foundation 1960, 1962, 1963, 1968, 1971, 1972, 1973, 1975, 1977. Used by permission.

Recommended Dewey Decimal Classification: 248.4
Suggested Subject Heading: CHRISTIAN LIFE

Library of Congress Catalog Card Number: 83-61158
ISBN: 0-88207-293-5

Contents

Foreword

Two thousand years ago the Apostle James observed that even though the tongue is a small part of the body, it can do enormous damage. And for two thousand years, millions of tongues have proven the truth of that statement. Regrettably, too many Christians are part of that number.

The Apostle Paul said to yield our members so they become weapons of righteousness. How should we do this? That's the purpose of this book—to help us have Spirit-controlled tongues that will serve God. I think you will be impressed to learn how much the Bible has to say on this subject and how skillfully Joe Stowell brings it all together.

Pastor Stowell writes from a background that not only enables him to handle the biblical material competently, but also to apply it pastorally. He probes deeply, but always kindly. The only way not to profit from this book would be to form a callous on your heart quickly and thickly!

CHARLES C. RYRIE

In Anticipation

Being in the ministry has made me acutely aware of the significance of words. Sermons leave no room for explanation or clarification once the benediction is said. Phrases assembled in the mill of my heart and mind are fed into the grid of a thousand experiences, backgrounds, philosophies, anxieties, and personalities. A word, a tone, a gesture, a turn of the head can mean so many different things to different people. If it weren't for the power of the Word and superintending work of the Spirit, I would lack the courage to preach.

People come to me broken by the words of others. I wonder how many times I've wounded with words and haven't even known it. I hear myself say things I wish I hadn't said and hear things said that I wish I'd never heard.

I have stood by bedsides where words were fitly spoken, words that brought comfort and peace. I have been with those who spoke words of forgiveness and love and have seen relationships healed. I have been loved by words and have loved with words. I know their warmth.

It is no wonder that words are important to God—they

convey so much. This book deals with God's view of what we say and is dedicated to bringing the joy of good words to His people. It is designed as a study. It may be better taken in bites and digested than consumed in one sitting.

Admittedly, writing a book on what to say and what not to say carries some inherent risks. Who will ever speak to me again? Let me assure my friends that I am still too busy working on my own words to evaluate theirs. Another risk is that some may assume that my speech will be consistently perfect. I beg for their patience.

Special recognition must go to:

- Several friends who spent their valuable time reviewing and sharing insightful suggestions concerning the content of this book
- The people of the Highland Park Baptist Church for their vision for this extended ministry
- Monalee Ferrero, my secretary, for both her skills and suggestions in the typing of this manuscript
- Charles Ryrie for his helpful evaluation of the manuscript

The effectiveness of this book has been enhanced by my wife's wise and faithful assistance. God has blessed my life with Martie. She is His wisely designed complement and my joy.

My prayer is that this book will be a healer and helper for the glory of God and the strength of His work.

To my friends Dave Haffey and Jim Reardon
whose words have been an encouragement to me.

1

A WORD'S WORTH

The "problem" tongue exposed

An insurance adjuster recently noted the unique way that people file reports on their claims when asked to describe their accidents in the fewest words possible:

"I pulled from the side of the road, glanced at my mother-in-law, and headed for the embankment."

"The pedestrian had no idea which way to run, so I ran over him."

"The guy was all over the road; I had to swerve a number of times before I hit him."

Communication. It is the process of expressing how we feel and what we think. It is impression as well. It is a tricky, risky piece in the puzzle of existence. Words can confuse, embarrass, and hurt. Conversely, they have the power to heal, encourage, help, and teach. Unfortunately, unless we are under the Holy Spirit's control, our words are more prone to hurt than to heal.

Words are often tragically destructive. Recently my favorite sports writer was analyzing a fine levied on a local baseball manager for verbally chewing out the commissioner. His column defended the manager by saying, "After all, they were just words."

Just words? There's no such thing. It's like saying, "After all, it's just an atom bomb!" The following testimony shows the destructive potential that words possess:

My junior high school had scheduled its annual operatic production. Talented students were quick to try out for the various parts. I was not so certain of my abilities and had decided that singing in an operetta wasn't really for me.

Then Mrs. Wilson, my music teacher, asked me to try out for the role of the black servant. It was not a coveted role, but it *did* have three solos.

I am certain that my audition was only mediocre. But Mrs. Wilson reacted as if she had just heard a choir of heavenly angels. "Oh, that was just beautiful. That was perfect. You are just right for the role. You will do it, won't you?" I accepted.

When the time came for the next year's operetta, most of the students who had played the leads the year before had graduated. And Mrs. Wilson had transferred to another school. In her place was a rather imposing figure who had an excellent singing voice and a sound knowledge of music theory.

As the tryouts began, I was ready. I felt confident that my talent was just what the operetta needed. With approximately 150 of my peers assembled, I knew everything would go well.

But if I live for an eternity I will never forget the words spoken on that day. When my audition was completed, the teacher asked, "Who told you you could sing?"

The timid youth of a year earlier was suddenly reborn. I was totally destroyed. Harsh words are bad enough under any circumstances. To a young idealistic boy, they can be devastating. From the time those six words were stated, it took eight years and the coaxing of my fiancee before my voice was raised in song again.

Words have tremendous weight. The pen really *is* mightier than the sword. It is not true that "names will never hurt me." Job said, "How long will you vex my soul and break me in pieces with words?" (Job 19:2, KJV) I must be constantly aware that my words to my children as their father, to my congregation as their pastor, and to my wife as her life partner carry impact. That's why God holds me accountable for my words (Matt. 12:36-37).

Devastating words aren't the only problem we have with our speech. Occasionally, our tongues simply succumb to the cascade of everyday pressures. A young mother recently sent this s.o.s. to me after an evening service.

Dear Pastor,

How do you control your tongue when: your schoolboy can't find his shoes and he's almost late for the bus, then the baby starts crying, the oatmeal starts to burn, and the phone rings? You answer the phone and tell your friend to please call back later. Quickly trying to salvage a little oatmeal for the crying baby, your other school-aged child that you sent upstairs 20 minutes ago to get dressed appears in the doorway still in her pajamas.

This is the everyday type situation where my mind as well as my tongue becomes unglued! Maybe you could touch on this Sunday nite.

Thanx,
Beth

In addition to stress from our everyday encounters, our words come under the pressure of our exposure to negative patterns of speech. Many of us are exposed to degrading speech on a daily basis. From the choice words of an angry boss to the crude and shaded language of prime time TV; in casual conversation with a neighbor to careless chatter among Christians; there is a steady exposure to corrupted communication. Unfortunately, our tongues often become a mimic of the input and, to our chagrin, the destructive words are out before we know it—occasionally in front of people who can't believe what they're hearing!

Whether it be well-meant confusion, careless destruction, survival in chaos, or subconscious submission to environmental patterns of speech, words can be destructive in three-dimensions. They are able to destroy our relationship with God, our relationship with those we treasure the most, and even our relationship with ourselves. Having a tongue is like having dynamite in our dentures—it must be reckoned with.

God's Word reflects the tremendous task that we face in transforming our tongues. James wrote, "No man can tame the tongue" (James 3:8). This statement is not included in James 3 to strike a note of despair or to encourage continued failure, but rather to let us know that self-initiated effort is of no avail. To make matters worse, we read that the tongue is "set on fire by hell" (v. 6). When it comes to transforming the tongue from a hellish fire to an instrument of constructive communication, we find ourselves up against a task of supernatural proportions. In the arena of transformed tongues, "our struggle is not against flesh and blood," but against an organized hierarchy of satanic power (Eph. 6:12).

Transforming our tongues requires supernatural strength. Victory demands taking up supernatural arms—being "strong in the Lord and in His mighty power" (v. 10). Being strong in the Lord is no mystical, hocus-pocus process. Being strong in the supernatural, victorious strength of the Lord has some solid resources that are available to us. These

resources are what Paul calls the armor of God (vv. 14-17).
The first piece of the armor is truth. Scripture teaches us that
the truth of God is our source of spiritual energy and growth
(Matt. 4:4; 1 Peter 2:2). As we discover and digest God's
Word, the indwelling Spirit transforms it into growth—growth
that produces spiritual, victorious strength.

God has blessed us with a wealth of truth in regard to the
tongue—truth that warns, convicts, and transforms us as we
permit it to take residence within us. One of the most instructive sections of truth on the tongue is James 3. In this passage, five principles unfold that make us aware of the gravity
of our words.

Principle 1: The Measure of Maturity

"We all stumble in many ways. If anyone is never at fault in
what he says, he is a perfect man, able to keep his whole body
in check" (James 3:2).

The word *stumble* means "to fall or to trip." What a
graphic picture of immaturity in our speech—tripping. Our
seven-week-old sheep dog, Paddington, trips over everything
in his path. His clumsy stumbling reflects his immaturity. A
stumbling tongue reflects our spiritual age as well. Unfortunately, we not only trip ourselves as we talk our way through
life, but we also trip others. Perhaps some of us feel quite
comfortable with our stumbling speech patterns because the
people around us tend to be "tongue-trippers" as well. We
may have assumed that the normal Christian experience is
to litter the landscape with saints felled by our words. After
all, doesn't everyone have trouble with their tongues? Our
spiritual maturity is not measured by the communication
patterns of those around us, but by the standards of God's
Word.

The word *perfect* literally means complete or mature. This
verse asserts that we are not mature until we stumble not in
word, being able to bring our entire body under control.

Certain skills are priority skills. If you master them, others come quite naturally. A marathon runner has no difficulty running a mile. A professional golfer can handle the two foot putts. And so it is with the tongue. If we master the tongue, we have the capacity to master other areas of our lives.

Have you ever seen someone revive a drowning victim with mouth-to-mouth resuscitation? What a thrill it would be to bring renewed life to our relationships by learning the skill of mouth-to-mouth maturity.

Principle 2: Small but Significant

"When we put bits into the mouths of horses to make them obey us, we can turn the whole animal. Or take ships as an example. Although they are so large and are driven by strong winds, they are steered by a very small rudder wherever the pilot wants to go. Likewise the tongue is a small part of the body, but it makes great boasts. Consider what a great forest is set on fire by a small spark" (James 3:3-5).

Wars that have claimed thousands of lives have been ignited by the tongue's spark. Marriages that once set sail on a joyous adventure have been steered onto the rocks by the rudder of a splintered tongue. After several years in the ministry, I cannot recall one counseling situation in which the problem was not either ignited or seriously complicated by negative words.

Termites are a terror! They are small and normally unseen creatures who chew their way through the accumulated equity of many homes. James says that the tongue is like that— small, but significant. He illustrates the significance of small things by citing a bit, a rudder, and a spark. He then concludes, "The tongue is a little member, and boasteth great things" (v. 5, KJV).

The kids on the block say it best. The tattletale is called "Mr. Bigmouth." That isn't a reference to the size of his mouth, but rather a pungent description of the heap of trouble that his little mouth produces.

Principle 3: Combustible Commodity

"The tongue also is a fire, a world of evil among the parts of the body. It corrupts the whole person, sets the whole course of his life on fire, and is itself set on fire by hell" (James 3:6).

The seriousness of the tongue's activity is revealed in the truth that it is "set on fire by hell." It is a "world of evil," literally an entire network of sin. We have an organized crime syndicate right in our mouths. Our tongues have the capacity to corrupt our entire being—nothing is exempt from the damage our tongues can cause.

Occasionally my wife and I have enjoyed the privilege of being with respected godly people. Though the encounters have always proven beneficial, more than once we have found ourselves surprised by their readiness to freely share the faults of others and thereby unconsciously tarnish their images.

We should remember that fire is one of the few forces that does irreparable damage. Fiery words often destroy relationships that, even when restored, are never the same again. Our families, our businesses, our churches, our friends, our enemies, our wealth, our security, our happiness, and our peace are all vulnerable to the defilement of the tongue. We should wear signs that say, "CAUTION: LIFE IS A COMBUSTIBLE COMMODITY—DOUSE YOUR TONGUE!"

Principle 4: A Wild and Deadly Beast

"All kinds of animals, birds, reptiles, and creatures of the sea are being tamed and have been tamed by man, but no man can tame the tongue. It is a restless evil, full of deadly poison" (James 3:7-8).

I get a kick out of how much effort we put into taming

animals. There is "elephant soccer," dogs that bark "Jingle-bells," chimps that communicate in sign language, birds that talk, and porpoises that "shoot baskets" better than I do.

Taming the tiger in our tongues must be a priority. By the Spirit's power, the tongue can be tamed for God's glory. If we do not bring it under the Spirit's control, it will be "full of deadly poison." When speaking of sinful mankind, Paul wrote, "The poison of vipers is on their lips" (Rom. 3:13).

In regions of South America there is a snake called the "Two-Step" snake. If it bites you, you take two steps and die. Its venom swiftly paralyzes your nervous system which stops your heart. Words can be like that. They have the potential to swiftly kill a relationship, paralyze love, poison minds, destroy faith, stain purity, and deface reputations.

Principle 5: The Double-Trouble Tongue

"With the tongue we praise our Lord and Father, and with it we curse men, who have been made in God's likeness. Out of the same mouth come praise and cursing. My brothers, this should not be. Can both fresh water and salt water flow from the same spring? My brothers, can a fig tree bear olives, or a grapevine bear figs? Neither can a salt spring produce fresh water" (James 3:9-12).

Someone has said that most tongues are tied in the middle, wagging at both ends. God's Word pictures it as a double tongue (1 Tim. 3:8). It's amazing how we can verbally poison one another all the way to church and as soon as we turn into the parking lot begin to speak out of the pious side of our mouths! We hardly finish singing the doxology and we are complaining about the usher who didn't put us in our favorite pew. "My brethren, these things ought not so to be" (James 3:10, KJV).

Even nature doesn't act so incongruously. It would be im-possible for our wells to send forth salt and fresh water, and for our fig trees to bear olives! If they did, we would reject them with disappointment. God might well ask us, "Can a 'new creation' (2 Cor. 5:17) send forth 'old words'?"

In these five principles James has categorized the tragic and shifty potential of the tongue. Step one to victory is to permit these truths to penetrate us. James rings a clear warning. A transformed tongue must be a top priority for those on the growth edge of discipleship.

James' warning, however, takes on added weight when we realize that many Christians are insensitive to the problems of destructive speech. We excuse one another with rationalizations such as, "Well, it's the truth, isn't it?" or "If they didn't want people to talk, they never should have done it." The most subtle excuse among Christians is, "Let me share this with you that we might pray more intelligently." This desensitization process has opened the floodgates to communication sins.

I understand that if you put a frog in a pan of cold water and place the pan on the stove, the frog will not jump out— but will slowly boil to death. It's not that the frog is dumb. It's that his nerve endings become desensitized in the heated water. The hotter the water becomes, the more numb his nerve endings become—until finally he is cooked.

Like the frog, we too can numb our spiritual nerve endings. By making careless communication an acceptable part of our lives, we assume that a carnal tongue is par for the spiritual course. When that happens, our churches, schools, homes, friendships, and relationships with God will all be victimized—cooked to death by our lack of sensitivity.

Sins like beguilement, deceit, lying, and false witness need to be understood from God's point of view. Social sins of the tongue, such as gossip and slander, must be checked. Verbal ego trips, such as boasting, flattery, and exaggeration, are clearly out of bounds. The cancer of a murmuring,

2

TO TELL THE TRUTH

*Beguilement, deceit, lying,
and false witness
destroy truth*

Mark Twain once quipped, "When in doubt, tell the truth. It will confound your enemies and astound your friends."

Truth telling has fallen on hard times. Since our culture has shifted to the ethics of expediency and self-advancement, falsehood is commonly seen as a virtue. As a result, many of us have come to feel better about lying.

In sales, a lie to sell is justifiable for the company's good. Even in religious philosophy, lying is not always considered wrong. Joseph Fletcher's system of situation ethics has so permeated our thinking that it is not uncommon to hear some religious leaders say that in certain situations lying would be virtuous.

Transforming non-truth from vice to virtue is representative of the great cultural shift in our thinking. To the modern American, wrong is not always wrong and right is not always right. Therefore, lying is not always wrong and telling the truth is not always right. Unfortunately, this undermining of the absolute value of truth has devastating consequences.

Truth has valuable allies. Trust, confidence, integrity, faith, security, and stability are unflinchingly loyal to her. When truth is disposed of, her allies leave with her. Conversely, falsehood is allied with suspicion, doubt, withdrawal, insecurity, conflict, resentment, and anger. When non-truth replaces truth, the friends of falsehood will always be present. Augustine said, "When regard for truth has been broken down or even slightly weakened, all things will remain doubtful."

This erosion of trust and confidence touches every relationship into which nontruth is injected. Homes are victimized, governments become suspect, media information is viewed with skepticism, and business relationships wear the shrouds of suspicion. No relationship can succeed, let alone survive, if it is based on that which is false.

Spiritual Consequences

Scripture demonstrates the serious spiritual consequences of tampering with the truth. A moratorium on lying is included in the Ten Commandments (Ex. 20:16). A lying tongue is included in the infamous list in Proverbs 6:17. When describing those whose lives will be judged in the Lake of Fire, God includes liars (Rev. 21:8). The psalmist, in aligning his life with truth, affirms, "I hate every wrong path" (Ps. 119:104). Scripture shows that God desires that truth would dwell within us (51:6). But why is truth so important to God?

Alignment. God's intense concern for truthfulness centers in His very nature. He is a "God of truth" (Ps. 31:5). God cannot lie (Titus 1:2).

Jesus Christ is "full of grace and truth" (John 1:14). The Holy Spirit is the "Spirit of truth" and His mission is to guide us into the truth (14:17; 16:13). All the ways of God are true (Ps. 25:10, KJV). "His works are done in truth" (33:4, KJV). The truth is the key to our worship (John 4:24). Therefore, our commitment to the truth aligns us with God, His nature, and His mode of operation. It is a matter of fellowship.

Reflection. Our very purpose in existing as God's children is to be conformed to the image of His Son (Rom. 8:29). We are redeemed to reflect His character. When we participate in falsehood, we abort the purpose of our redemption and tarnish the reflection of His glory through us. If God is truth, then we too must portray truth to accurately reflect God's image in our lives.

Submission. God's Word commands us to speak the truth—regardless of the cost. "The righteous hate what is false" (Prov. 13:5). Paul wrote, "Do not lie to each other" (Col. 3:9). Nowhere in Scripture does God grant exemption from these commands. They are absolute. Our consciences cannot be clear before God and our joy cannot be full if we get involved with that which is false. Truth-telling is a matter of submission to God's will.

Many have attempted to categorize the distortion of truth. For our study let's look at four categories that we need to understand.

Beguilement

One morning while leaving for the office, I noticed that someone had thrown a beer can on my front lawn. I picked it up, took it to the garbage can, lifted the lid, and threw it away. Then it hit me! *What will the garbage men think? A beer can tumbling out of the minister's garbage can?* The whole incident sent my mind racing as I drove to the office.

Our quickness to conclude wrongly is a subtle trap. Subtle, because it victimizes us when we have no intention to be deceived or to deceive. Yet we are quick to conclude wrongly and often proceed to share our false conclusions with all who will listen. That is beguilement.

I recall discovering that some money was missing from the church office. Immediately a suspect's name and face came to mind. Of course, who else would have done it? As I mused over the situation, I caught myself degrading the person, planning how I would confront him, and wondering who I should tell so that they could "pray about the situation." I felt my anger building. My judgmental spirit had pronounced the verdict. As the staff discussed the "case of the missing cash," I was quick to indict the guilty party. My spirit had developed a negative focus and just seeing "the thief" aroused a negative response in me.

Then it was as though the Spirit tapped me on the shoulder and said, "What if you are wrong? Do you have all the facts?" It occurred to me that even our secular system of justice claims a man innocent until proven guilty.

Beguilement is the sin of sharing false conclusions. It is to delude or be deluded. And though often done innocently, it is devastating. It plants seeds of mistrust, doubt, confusion, and irreparably destroys reputations.

There are indeed two sides to every story. Being careless with the details and having insufficient facts are the stuff of which false accusations are made. We must learn to resist the temptation to draw conclusions until sufficient information is in.

How can we fortify ourselves against this temptation to misjudge and pass along false information? Several biblical suggestions will be of help. We must develop:

- A *patient spirit* that suspends judgment until sufficient facts are verified (Gal. 5:22)
- A *love* that believes the best until facts prove otherwise (1 Cor. 13:6-7)
- A faith that *prays* the situation into the courts of heaven where an "all-knowing God" promises to judge all men righteously (1 Peter 1:17)
- A willingness to *protect* others by encouraging those who are sharing false accusations to reserve judgment until sufficient facts are in (1 Cor. 13:4)

- A boldness *to go* directly (if necessary) to those involved to clarify the facts (Matt. 18:15)

The alternative is to become like spiritual jackrabbits who jump to all the wrong conclusions, leaving in our trails broken lives and relationships that we could have protected and healed.

Deceit

It's amazing how facts can be arranged to manipulate. Read the following phrase carefully: *Woman without her man is a beast*! Now read the same words again: *Woman—without her, man is a beast*! What made the difference? Neither the facts nor the word order changed. But a variation in punctuation totally changed the concept.

The tremendous power of deceit is demonstrated in Genesis 3:1-6. Through deceit Satan not only gained control of Eve, but also caused Adam to sin and imposed the curse of sin on all of God's creation (Rom. 5:12).

Satan's ploy began with a question, "Did God really say, 'You must not eat from any tree in the garden'?" (Gen. 3:1) At this point Satan was telling the truth. But Satan's presentation of the facts led Eve to believe that God was restrictive and stingy. To her, serving God was now perceived as enslavement. She concluded that God had kept her from experiencing the completeness of life around her.

In retrospect, God had said, "You are *free* to eat from *any tree* in the garden; but you must not eat from the tree of the knowledge of good and evil" (2:16-17).* After reading God's words to Adam, I am struck with the generosity and the love of God. Adam and Eve could eat from every tree in the garden except one—what a kind and generous Creator!

---

*Italics are used in Bible verses for author's emphasis.

Satan told the truth in a way that deceived Eve into thinking wrongly about God. He twisted the facts to ultimately gain advantage over Eve and all the created order of God. God's Word calls it deceit (3:13; 2 Cor. 11:3). It is a powerful tool in the tactical warfare of Satan.

Deception has become a widely used technique for manipulation, self-advancement, and self-protection. It is evident in those who, living in known sin, carry the facade of pious behavior through the halls of the church. From the businessman who carefully words the fine print to cloud the true commitment being made on the dotted line; to the pastor who purposely uses Scripture to manipulate a congregation; to the professor who selectively chooses statistics to prove his own point; deceit is a prevalent reality. It is a destroyer of trust. It is a menace to stable, growing relationships.

Legal restraints such as "truth-in-advertising," "truth-in-lending," and "truth-in-testimony" demonstrate how prevalent deceit is in our way of life. The "credibility gap" is a result of the undermining of our confidence through deceit in media, government, business, politics, and tragically, even in the church.

The writer of Proverbs says, "Food gained by fraud tastes sweet to a man, but he ends up with a mouth full of gravel" (Prov. 20:17). Deceit is the sign of a wicked heart (12:20).

Both beguilement and deceit tamper with, twist, and distort the truth. Lying, on the other hand, is the direct communication of non-truth.

Lying

Coconut has always been my weakness. For me, there is a direct connection between coconut and my early impressions about lying.

One day after school I found a bag of shredded coconut in the kitchen cupboard. I yielded and ate. How was I to know that my mother intended to use it for a cake she was baking that night? Upon discovering that her cupboards had been vandalized, my mother called my two sisters and me to the kitchen and demanded a confession. My sisters swore their innocence. I, of course, followed suit.

When my father came home, he sat all of us down in the living room. We each affirmed our innocence again. Mark Twain once said, "The principle difference between a cat and a lie is that a cat has only nine lives." Well, I was at nine and counting when my dad opened his Bible and read that liars have their place in the Lake of Fire (Rev. 21:8). That did it. I could hold out no longer and I sheepishly confessed.

Since that day I have had a deep respect for the seriousness of lying. I learned that "those who cook up stories usually find themselves in hot water." It wasn't until later in life, however, that I discovered *why* lying was such a serious matter to God. Scripture relates several realities about a lying tongue that should give every believer cause for concern.

Lying—the base of Satan's strategy. In Genesis 3, not only did Satan *deceive* Eve about God's goodness, but he also *lied* to Eve about God and His Word. He said to Eve, "You will not surely die" (Gen. 3:4). That was a clear communication of non-truth. God had said, "when you eat of [the tree] you will surely die" (2:17). Lying was a central part of Satan's strategy.

It is not surprising that non-truth is still Satan's main method of operation today. He has pervaded our culture with the lie that there are no consequences to sin. His system tells us that wealth and possessions will make us happy. He lies to us about God by saying, "If God is good, why did He permit your parents to divorce? Why is there so much suffering?"

His lie puts on clerical robes and says, "Be as good as you can and you'll go to heaven. Just be sincere." The non-truth system says that man is the result of a chance evolutionary process. Satan tells us that success is measured by wealth, cars, and houses; freedom is found in doing anything we want to do.

Lying against the truth is the strength of Satan's system. Not only does he lie, but his desire is that we will lie as well. When we lie, we tie into and support his program. That's exactly what Christ inferred when He said to the Pharisees who had lied about Him, "You belong to your father, the devil, and you want to carry out your father's desire. He was a murderer from the beginning, not holding to the truth, for there is no truth in him. When he lies, he speaks his native language, for he is a liar and the father of lies" (John 8:44). Non-truth is the language of the world system. James warns us that "friendship with the world is hatred toward God. Anyone who chooses to be a friend of the world becomes an enemy of God" (James 4:4).

Lying—part of the believer's past. Lying is a product of the flesh. It is a part of what we used to be. "Do not lie to each other, since you have taken off your old self with its practices and have put on the new self, which is being renewed in knowledge in the image of its Creator" (Col. 3:9-10). Our newness aligns us with Christ and with His truth. No wonder Proverbs 12:22 says, "The Lord detests lying lips, but He delights in men who are truthful." The one who enjoys fellowship with God "speaks the truth from his heart and has no slander on his tongue, who does his neighbor no wrong and casts no slur on his fellow man" (Ps. 15:2-3).

Even though lying is the base of Satan's strategy and a part of our spiritual past, it lingers as an ever present tendency within us. Lies that serve self and lies that serve others are often found on the tips of our tongues.

Lies that serve self. Why do we lie so readily? Lying is a quick and easy way to gain advantage, protection, and promotion of personal interests. We lie to catch people's attention and to promote ourselves in people's esteem. We lie to get rich and we lie to get elected. We lie to protect our reputations and we lie to escape punishment. Most lies are dedicated servants of self.

In my first pastorate, the Sunday School superintendent reminded me to order the Sunday School books so they would be on hand for the new quarter. I promised I would, but I promptly forgot. The next Sunday morning as I walked through the foyer, I met the superintendent. He asked if I had ordered the material. In a flash, I answered him and found myself overcome with guilt. I had lied. I lied to protect my reputation. After all, how could I, the pastor, have forgotten? How could I be that careless with his needs? As I walked on to my office, I was annoyed at how quickly I had responded with a lie. It wasn't premeditated—it was automatic. Self-interest was still alive and well in my being.

As I settled in at my desk, the Holy Spirit urged me to clear up the matter before I preached. I was in turbulence. Could I admit to the superintendent that I had lied? Could I live without admitting it? The flesh and the Spirit were waging all out internal war (Gal. 5:17). The superintendent would never know the difference if I didn't tell him. I could call immediately Monday morning and have the order rushed. If it didn't come right away, I could always blame the publishing house. If I admitted it, my credibility would be destroyed.

Ultimately the rationalizations of the flesh proved to be of no avail. I knew I was wrong. I knew that I had to confess—to God and to the superintendent. If I didn't, my relationship with him would be tainted with guilt and fear. I knew that lying, even if undiscovered, drives a wedge between the best of friends. If I didn't make it right, my preaching would be from the heart of a hypocrite harboring known sin.

Thankfully, upon seeking his forgiveness, I found the man

to be graciously forgiving. My spirit was free—I had won back a friend and deepened a relationship.

Lies that serve others. A greater challenge to our commitment to truth is found in the cultural mood of lying to protect. At first this may seem to be a valid exception to the righteous goal of truthfulness. We've all heard the war stories of Jewish children who were asked by the Nazi soldiers if their parents were home. From the weighty consideration of that kind of a situation to the common "social lies" that keep everyone smiling, we tend to excuse certain lies for their social benefit.

Admittedly, it is sometimes hard to tactfully apply the truth. What do you say when you see a newborn, red, wrinkled baby in the hospital? How do you respond when you're asked to admire that new dress, hat, or tie? We often tell "little white lies." The phrase itself is a contradiction; lying is never little and always a part of the darkness! As someone once said, "Those who are given to white lies soon become color blind."

This is not to say that we are to "brutally" speak the truth. God's Word commands us to speak the truth in love (Eph. 4:15). The truth must travel with mercy, gentleness, understanding, and grace. There is no virtue in glorifying God by telling the truth and at the same time destroying the glory of God's grace with an insensitive spirit. As Pascal said, "The abuse of truth ought to be as much punished as the introduction of falsehood."

We need to learn to pray for wisdom in our speech (James 1:5). We should train ourselves to search for the truth in a given situation. For instance, we can say that the red, wrinkled baby is precious (they all are); or that there's something to be commended about that dress—the color, the fit, the style. As Proverbs says, "A man finds joy in giving an apt reply—and how good is a timely word!" (Prov. 15:23) "The heart of the righteous weighs its answers, but the mouth of the wicked gushes evil" (v. 28). As Paul said, "Let your conversation be always full of grace, seasoned with salt, so that you may know how to answer everyone" (Col. 4:6).

Proponents of lying to serve others often point to the incident of Rahab, who protected the spies by lying to the soldiers. She is modeled as a righteous forerunner of those who lie today to protect others from danger. Her faith is commended in the New Testament and, on initial reading, we might conclude that her lie was not only right, but blessed of God. If that is true, then prohibitions against lying are not absolute and we are left to determine the situations in which lying may have redeeming social value. The ramifications of taking the absolute status of truth away, of claiming that non-truth can accomplish righteousness, are profound.

We should keep in mind that Rahab was a pagan with no awareness of God's Law. I doubt if we would be comfortable in applying her perception of righteousness to our code of biblical ethics today.

But there is more to understand about Rahab's lie. Initially, Rahab's *faith* is commended in the New Testament (Heb. 11:31), *not her lie*. Her faith was a response to the news she had received about God's blessing on the Children of Israel as they had crossed the Red Sea and won great military victories (Josh. 2:9-11). It was faith in the reality and the power of the God of Israel that saved her. Her *lying* was actually a lapse in her faith. Had her faith in God been complete, Rahab would have concluded that God could protect the spies without her lie.

In reality, Rahab's lie precluded God's opportunity to supernaturally intervene as He has done so many times (the Red Sea, Daniel in the lion's den, the Resurrection, Peter in prison). Later on, the two spies hid in the mountains and were hunted for *three days* by soldiers from Jericho who were familiar with the terrain. Miraculously, they were not found (v. 22).

Much of the speculation in this text assumes that it would have been "bad" for the spies to have been found. That is a shallow assumption. God often uses what seems tragic to us to work great good. The worst that could have happened was for them to be killed. For those who serve God, that may be His plan. The early martyrs refused to lie to save their lives and it was through their blood that the first century took notice of a faith that was worth dying for. As Paul says, death is a door to all that is "better by far" (Phil. 1:23).

Rahab's lie does not prove that lying is acceptable to God. If anything, Rahab's lie precluded God's opportunity to exercise several options that were open to Him, options that could have produced greater glory.

God's absolutes in regard to truthfulness must be seen in the scope of His supernatural, sovereign abilities to bring about His glory even, if necessary, through human tragedy. It is our responsibility to obey and His responsibility to "write the last chapter." It is a humanistic imposition on our Christianity to assume that we should do what is wrong to help God do what is right.

If anything, Rahab illustrates that God is a forgiving God who is willing to mercifully use even our disobedience for His glory. To use Rahab as an excuse for our lies violates Paul's command, "Shall we continue in sin, that grace may abound? God forbid" (Rom. 6:1-2, KJV).

False Witness

A particular sin against the truth is the sin of bearing false witness. Though the term *false witness* can be applied to any false testimony, it specifically refers to those who bear false testimony against another person, often for some personal gain. In a plot to gain an herb garden for King Ahab, Jezebel found two "worthless men" to lie about Naboth. As a result, he was stoned to death, and a sulking king got his herb garden (1 Kings 21:1-16). At the crucifixion of Christ, the High Priest brought in two "false witnesses" to testify against the Lord (Matt. 26:60-61). Whether to gain a garden or to crucify one who threatens your status and position, bearing false witness is a serious offense before God. In fact, when God included lying in the Decalogue, He called it "false witness."

This sin is of particular consequence in that it strikes injury, often irreparable, to innocent people, their reputations, and their families. It is a violent use of the tongue. It had the power to kill Naboth and to crucify Christ. Is it any wonder that God says, "A false witness will not go unpunished, and he who pours out lies will not go free"? (Prov. 19:5)

Beguilement, deceit, lying, and false witness are all means whereby Satan can defeat God's glory in us and through us. It is through these patterns of falsehood that he enlists us into the network of his "non-truth system."

Non-truth is a participant in every sin that Satan promotes. Whether it be lying to cover marital unfaithfulness or the destruction of a godly reputation by beguilement; whether deceiving to gain unjust business advantage, or bearing of false witness to carry out some selfish scheme; tampering with the truth supports, promotes, and protects the welfare of sin. Can you think of one sin where non-truth isn't a natural by-product or companion? It is the glue, the lifeblood of Satan's system.

Oliver Wendell Holmes said, "Sin has many tools, but a lie is the handle that fits them all."

3

MALICIOUSLY SPEAKING

Gossip and slander— catastrophic cousins

It was a great story! I found myself telling it every time I got the chance. It was true—I thought.

Someone in our church had a couple of elderly aunts who wanted to go to New York City. They had been warned what an evil place it was. In fact, their friends tried to talk them out of it. With the possibility of robbery, mugging, rape, or even murder lurking in every corner they were advised to stay home.

Undaunted, they went anyway. After checking into a fancy downtown hotel, they promptly made their way to the elevator. The door opened and there stood a large, stern-looking man wearing sunglasses and a white suit. A leashed Doberman Pinscher stood at his side. The ladies glanced nervously at each other and got on. No sooner had the elevator doors closed than the man in hushed tones commanded, "Sit!" To his amazement, the ladies both sank to the floor. As the elevator stopped, the man and his dog made their way past the sitting spinsters who then continued their ride up.

Upon checking out of the hotel, the ladies found that their room had been paid for. A note was attached to the bill. It read, "Ladies, you gave me the best laugh of my life. Your room's on me! Reggie Jackson."

I took great delight in sharing that story with friends. A group of professional baseball players thought it was the funniest thing they had ever heard. Then one evening as I told it to a group of couples, someone said, "I just read about that in *People* magazine. It's a rumor. Reggie Jackson emphatically denies it. He never wears white suits!" To say the least, I was embarrassed. I had been caught red-handed with a rumor in my mouth.

More devastating, however, are the rumors that destroy people. A frantic mother wrote to Ann Landers asking what to do about the rumor being spread that her 16-year-old daughter was pregnant. The mother wondered if perhaps she should transfer her daughter to another high school. Ann Landers suggested that she shouldn't switch schools. Instead, she should let time prove the rumor false. It sounded like good advice. But then the scenario developed in my mind that if she stayed, someone would say, "She had an abortion." Once rumors begin, it's tough to win!

Rumors, whether true or false, are devastating for many reasons—one of them being that they are irretrievable. The story is told of a young man during the Middle Ages who was sent to a monk. He said, "I've sinned by telling slanderous statements about someone. What should I do?" The monk replied, "Put a feather on every doorstep in town." The young man did just that. He then came back to the monk, wondering if there was anything else that he should do. The monk told him, "Go back and pick up all those feathers." The young man replied excitedly, "That's impossible! By now the wind will have blown them all over town!" Said the monk, "So has your slanderous word become impossible to retrieve."

Spiritually, many who have sinned find that after they are drawn back to God and experience full forgiveness, the story of their sins remains alive and well in many minds.

Rumors are the vehicles that turn life into a demolition derby, and gossip and slander are the tracks on which they travel. The tracks of gossip and slander are paved with careless, idle chatter as well as the malicious, intentional sharing of bad reports. From where does the fuel for this demolition derby come? Malicious speech comes from the central source of all sin—the promotion of self. Gossip and slander feed on our natural self-orientation in at least six ways.

First is the self-orientation of curiosity. Some of us look for and listen to "news" just because of our natural curiosity. Obviously, our curiosity can be constructive. A curiosity to know God and His will is a spiritual plus. Yet, if our curiosity plays into the scheme of seeking, bearing, and disseminating harmful information, then we have misused our natural instincts and have fed ourselves on the well-being of others. It's not by accident that busybodies (people whose curiosity has gone wild) are linked with tattlers (those who share what their unchecked curiosity has discovered) in the same context (1 Tim. 5:13).

Second, 1 Timothy 5:13 states that people with time on their hands may be prone to malicious speech. In speaking about widows' temptations, Paul says they are "*idle,* going about from house to house" (v. 13). Today, for some, the wandering from house to house has been enhanced by the telephone. People who are slothful may easily become slanderous. But people who are constructively busy with their own responsibilities have little time to be busy about the responsibilities of others.

Third, a desire to be the center of attention often is the impetus for slander or gossip. It captures attention to say, "Did you hear?", "Well, I really shouldn't say this, but," or

"If you can keep a secret." It's a stroke to the ego to have everyone listening intently when we speak. Some of us feed on the attention—unfortunately at the expense of others.

Fourth, the proneness to elevate ourselves over others often stimulates negative speech. If I can say something derogatory about you, I feel better about myself. At least I'm not as bad as you are! As Will Durant said, "To speak ill of others is a dishonest way of praising ourselves."

Fifth, malicious words are often spawned by bitterness. Selfishly withholding forgiveness opens the door to a vengeful spirit. Slander is a tool of revenge. The slander we pour out against those who have hurt us is the natural vent of our hostile spirit. In fact, unresolved bitterness will be transferred to other situations that remind us of the events that angered us in the first place. This makes us vulnerable to lives characterized by slander.

Sixth, we are prone to speak of negative things because it soothes our own anxieties. Misery still loves company. That's why bad news moves by express while good news hardly gets down the track. Good news about others heightens our anxieties about our own problems.

In God's Word, several terms are used to describe this destructive pattern of speech; they primarily carry two connotations. One connotation is *idle chatter that is damaging to another's integrity and reputation*. This is not always malicious in its intent, but it is always damaging. This concept is translated in Scripture as "whisper" and "gossip."

The second connotation is the *intentional, malicious communication of bad reports*. This concept is normally translated "slander."

Gossip

R.G. LeTourneau, the owner of a large earth moving equipment company, often told this story: "We used to have a scraper known as the model 'G.' Somebody asked one of our salesmen one day what the 'G' stood for. The salesman was pretty quick on the trigger, and so after thinking a few seconds, replied, 'Well, I guess the 'G' stands for gossip, because like gossip, this machine moves a lot of dirt, and moves it fast!"

Both the Hebrew and Greek words for gossip are picturesque. One of the Old Testament words refers to "going about from one to another" (Prov. 11:13). Hence, our word "talebearing." The concept of "whispering that is damaging" is the essence of the word as it is used in Proverbs 16:28, 18:8 and 26:20, 22.

The New Testament word continues the thought of whispering. One lexicographer describes it as "secret attacks on a person's character." When you pronounce the Greek word for gossip, you begin with the sound p-s-s-s. P-s-s-t is often how we characterize hushed communication.

Though whispering is not always bad, it is always used in a negative context in Scripture. It denotes confidential information, non-public information, exclusivism, secretive behavior, and shame. In Scripture, whispering becomes a figurative expression for the sin of gossip, which unfortunately is not always done in a whisper.

God's Word teaches that a gossip is untrustworthy and cannot keep a secret (Prov. 11:13). Gossips often betray confidential information. Their information is not worthy of trust because they tend to add "frills" to the story to make it more interesting.

The person who gossips is to be avoided (20:19). When we hear gossip, we add unneeded information to our mental notebook. These negative thoughts give Satan a foothold in our lives. Hearing soon becomes telling—for some, "gossip in" means "gossip out!"

Gossip adds fuel to the fire (26:20). Gossips have a great ability to keep division and strife at a fever pitch by sharing unforgettable information (18:8; 26:22). These "juicy morsels" stay with us, permanently staining our perceptions of and appreciation for those whom we are hearing about. If we would stop spreading information about feuding factions and start praying, the fight might fizzle.

Gossip separates the closest of friends (16:28). When you hear gossip about a friend, it begins to drive a wedge between the two of you. It builds a barrier of suspicion and doubt. Conversely, if my friend gossips to me about someone else, I begin to doubt my friend's loyalty. After all, if he gossips *to* me, maybe he will gossip *about* me.

The gossiper disqualifies himself for fellowship with God and shows his lack of knowledge of God (Ps. 15:3; Rom. 1:28-30). Realizing that God knows, that He cares, and that He can deal with the situation gives us peace when we leave the situation with Him. If we know Him, we can commit the news to "Him who judges justly" (1 Peter 2:23) and love our neighbors as ourselves (Matt. 22:39).

We all know we shouldn't gossip. Yet our thirst for the "news" (both hearing and telling) at times seems insatiable, so we devise ways of sharing it that salve our consciences. Will Rogers quipped, "The only time people dislike gossip is when you gossip about them."

Slander

Next of kin to gossip is slander. While gossip is often done in the context of idle, careless chatter, slander is the open, intentional sharing of damaging information.

The Jews of the intertestamental period called the slanderous tongue "the third tongue." Third because it is fatal to three sets of people—to those who *speak* the slander, to those who *listen* to it, and to those *about* whom it is spoken.

Slander is pictured in both Hebrew and Greek in several definitive ways. The word used in the Old Testament to speak of slander (Ps. 31:13; Prov. 10:18; 25:10) is used in the more neutral sense of *bad reports* in general. It is used when Joseph told his father of the wickedness of his brothers (Gen. 37:2) and when the 10 spies brought back a negative report about the Promised Land (Num. 13:32; 14:36-37). This same word is translated by the Hebrew lexicon to mean "to defame" or to strip one of his positive reputation.

Another Hebrew word for slander literally means "to blemish or to fault" (Ps. 50:20). It is interesting that the Old Testament word for *foot* is the root word for the word translated both "spy" and "slander." Obviously, some people thrive so much on slander that they search for information and, as the lexicon says, "go about maliciously as slanderers" (2 Sam. 19:27; Ps. 15:3).

In the New Testament, the word for slander is comprised of two words. One meaning "against" and the other meaning "to speak." A slanderer is one who speaks against another (James 4:11; 1 Peter 2:1).

Interestingly, the word for devilish or diabolic is translated "slander" in the *King James Version* (1 Tim. 3:11) and "malicious talkers" in the *New International Version*. A deacon's wife is not to engage in slanderous (literally diabolic), malicious speech.

Grouping these nuances of slander together, we discover that slander is characterized by bad reports that blemish or defame a person's reputation. Slander characterizes a wicked, godless heart (Ps. 50:16-23; Rom. 1:28-30). Slander is a direct violation of God's Law (Lev. 19:16).

> Brothers, do not slander one another. Anyone who speaks against his brother or judges him speaks against the law and judges it. When you judge the law, you are not keeping it, but sitting in judgment on it. There is only one Lawgiver and Judge, the One who is able to save and destroy. But you—who are you to judge your neighbor? (James 4:11-12)

Slander disqualifies us for fellowship with God (Ps. 15:1-3). When we destroy with our tongues those whom God loves and is seeking to restore, we place ourselves in opposition to God and His purpose.

Not only does slander alienate us spiritually, but it also brings God's "silencing" work into our lives (Ps. 101:5). If we refuse to keep our tongues from slander then God, in His disciplining grace, will bring pressures to stop us (Prov. 3:11-12).

Late one night I was listening to a radio preacher as he was maligning his congregation for hurting the testimony of Christ with their words. He said, "I can understand why a hungry man would steal to eat, and I can understand why a man whose mother-in-law moved in would leave home. But I can't understand why any Christian I know would ever speak like that! If I were the Lord, I'd give you throat cancer right now!" I'm not sure that's what God intends for us. But I do know that He has many creative ways to effect a silencing work in our lives.

If we slander someone, we run the risk of being branded as a slanderer for the rest of our lives (25:9-10). The word for "betray a confidence" is the Hebrew word for slander. While it is true that sharing confidential information is often slanderous, one who tells slanderous secrets gets a reputation as a slanderer. Bad reputations are hard to live down.

Slander boomerangs (30:10). Slander can evoke the anger of those who hear it and of those whom we are slandering. Have you ever heard someone say, "I don't think you should say that about them"? How embarrassing. How convicting. Slandering others leaves us open to be criticized as a slanderer. It opens the possibility that someone will slander us.

Several disruptive realities accompany slander. David says that terror, conspiracy, and plotting are the destructive bedfellows of slander (Ps. 31:13). Slander surrounds itself with mistrust, doubt, exaggeration, and pride. It is an unfitting companion to a believer who wants to grow spiritually and reflect God's glory.

Gossip and slander are obviously serious violations of God's will. Why, then, are they so prevalent? Perhaps we have neutralized ourselves with "good" excuses. Several myths surround the social sport of telling tales. Recognizing them will help us to extricate this cancer from our conversation.

The first myth is that these are "women's" sins. While it is true that in two Bible references, the sins of slander and gossip are related to women (1 Tim. 3:11; 5:13), Scripture nowhere promotes the notion that men aren't just as guilty as women. The only difference is that men call it "shooting the breeze," "shop talk," or better yet, "problem solving."

The second myth is that if the information is true, it's "OK" to tell it. Nothing could be further from the truth. The issue is not whether the information is true or false, but whether it is harmful or confidential. The standard for what we speak about is clearly given in Romans 14:19: "Let us therefore make every effort to do what leads to peace and to mutual edification." "Do not let any unwholesome talk come out of your mouths, but only what is helpful for building others up according to their needs, that it may benefit those who listen" (Eph. 4:29).

The third myth is that "this problem needs a lot of prayer." While that may be true, the destructive communication is usually prefaced by, "Let me tell you this so that you can pray more intelligently."

Myth four relates to the unspoken desire for deeper relationships. Somehow we think that sharing confidential or negative information about another person will enhance the depth of the relationship with the one we are talking to. In fact, some relationships would never exist if it weren't for a common enemy to talk about. As we have learned, these communication traits don't deepen relationships; they ultimately separate them (Prov. 16:28).

The fifth myth is that "the ones I tell certainly won't tell anyone else." After all, they said they wouldn't. So did you!

We must strip away these myths and ask, What can we do with damaging information? God's Word gives us four options:

1. Take it to God in prayer and leave the matter with Him (1 Peter 5:7). There are some matters that are beyond our abilities to cope with or resolve. If we must talk about them, it should be to God.

2. Go directly to the one we have heard this about in a spirit of meekness and restoration (Matt. 18:15; Gal. 6:1). Unfortunately, the one who is being talked about is often the last one to hear the story. As one person said, "I was the talk of the town and didn't even know it." After getting that person's point of view, we may even have a new perspective on the information.

3. Take the information to one who is in a place of authority to rectify the situation (Matt. 18:15-17; Rom. 13:1-5).

4. Seek to protect the victim of the slander (Prov. 10:12). The Genesis account of Noah's family's response to his drunken nakedness graphically illustrates our responsibility. After the Flood, Noah was found naked in a drunken stupor in his tent. His son Ham "saw his father's nakedness and told his two brothers outside" (Gen. 9:22). The brothers had a different response. They took a blanket and walked backward into the tent so that they wouldn't see Noah's nakedness and covered him up (v. 23).

We, like Ham, have the option to reveal all we know about others, or, like Shem and Japeth, to show love by covering their shame. "Love covers all wrongs. He who covers over an offense promotes love, but whoever repeats the matter separates close friends" (Prov. 10:12; 17:9). "Love does no harm to its neighbor" (Rom. 13:10).

If we don't dismiss gossip and slander from our conversations, we become like social cannibals who devour one another. To hear some of us talk, we might conclude that we live by the ethic, "Eat thy neighbor," instead of the kingdom truth, "Love thy neighbor as thyself."

"You, my brothers, were called to be free. But do not use your freedom to indulge the sinful nature; rather, serve one another in love. The entire Law is summed up in a single command: 'Love your neighbor as yourself.' If you keep on biting and devouring each other, watch out or you will be destroyed by each other" (Gal. 5:13-15).

4
THE EGO IN OUR MOUTHS

Boasting, flattery, and exaggeration

Ego. We all have one. It's the part of me that is interested in me. It is that inner drive to be recognized and satisfied. It's one of the strongest driving forces in our beings. It's no wonder that it shows up in our mouths.

Though men seem to flaunt theirs more publicly, women possess their fair share of ego as well. None of us would function well without one. We all need enough ego to care about success, how we look, and how we feel about ourselves. Ego simply needs a control factor. Scripture tells us that the control factor is the Word of God and the indwelling Spirit (Eph. 5:18). The Spirit-controlled ego becomes a very productive instrument in the hand of God. It becomes the part of us that cares about spiritual success, being accepted before God, and serving our fellow man.

However, when ego is left to roam uncontrolled, it gets us into all kinds of trouble. Part of that trouble is made in our mouths. At least three sins of the tongue are revealed by our unchecked egos. They are boasting, flattery, and exaggeration.

Do not get drunk on wine, which leads to debauchery. Instead be filled w/the Spirit

Boasting

Boasting is a relatively popular social sport. Otherwise dull parties often thrive on our bigger and better boasts! The boaster is the guy who keeps the conversation circulating around himself and his accomplishments.

On the surface, boasting may seem like an innocent pastime. After all, "If you've got it, flaunt it." Some of us have come to realize that if we don't praise ourselves, no one will.

These shallow excuses notwithstanding, boasting is social suicide. Even the basic rules of communication dictate that we talk about the interests of others and not of ourselves. By bringing attention to his own glory, a boaster aborts the very purpose of redemption, which is to bring glory to God (1 Cor. 6:19-20). There are three pointed descriptions of those who boast.

The Inflated Zero. "Do nothing out of selfish ambition or vain conceit, but in humility consider others better than yourselves" (Phil. 2:3). The word for "vain conceit" comes from two Greek words meaning empty and glory. Vain conceit is the glorification of emptiness—the promotion of our "zeroness." God says that in our sinful natures there dwells nothing that is good (Rom. 7:18). Even our finest efforts aside from Him have the value of "filthy rags" (Isa. 64:6). Jesus said, "Apart from Me you can do nothing" (John 15:5). When I bring glory to myself it is then the glory of my emptiness. We should remember that empty barrels make the most noise.

No matter how big my zero is, it's still a zero. When I boast of myself, it is nothing more than the enlargement of my emptiness. It is vain conceit. My life, my works, and all that I am only take on meaning in and through Christ. "I have been crucified with Christ and I no longer live, but Christ lives in me. The life I live in the body, I live by faith in the Son of God, who loved me and gave Himself for me" (Gal.

Phil 2:3 - Do nothing out of selfish ambition or vain conceit, but in humility consider others better than yourselves. For I have the desire to do what is good, but I cannot carry it out

Rom 7:19 - I know that nothing good lives in me, that is, in my sinful nature.

Isaiah 64:6 - All of us have become like one who is unclean and all our righteous acts are like filthy rags. we all shrivel up like a leaf & like the wind our sins sweep us away.

2:20). When something good is done in me, it is of Him and not of me.

A seminary classmate of mine was a teller at a bank in Dallas. As he was doing some paperwork at his window, he noticed our professor of Hebrew at the next teller's window. At the close of the transaction, the professor stepped away from the window and counted his money. Realizing that he had been given too much cash, he stepped back to the window and told the teller. She counted the money and said, "My, you're an honest man." He carefully replied, "It's not that I'm an honest man; it's that Jesus Christ has changed my life." He knew that all that was good in him was of Christ and he tactfully gave God the credit. A boaster has no such perception.

The Wandering Quack. In the Old West, covered wagons would roll into town and, from the backs of the wagons, cures were sold to remedy all ills. From consumption to gout to "whatever ailed 'ya'," one bottle did it all. People gullibly bought, and the wagon disappeared into the sunset. These early American medicine men claimed to deliver more than they could. The Bible would classify them as braggarts.

The word translated *brag* in James 4:16 literally means a "wandering quack." A braggart boasts about things that he can't control and promises more than he can deliver. The context relates it to those who say, "Today or tomorrow we will go to this or that city, spend a year there, carry on business and make money" (v. 13). But we do not have ultimate control over what we can or cannot do. God sovereignly guides our courses of life. "Instead, you ought to say, 'If it is the Lord's will, we will live and do this or that'" (v. 15). This puts God in His proper role as the true governor of the affairs of our lives.

If any of us succeed, it is by God's careful and wise design. If we boast in our own abilities, then we speak as though there were no God. Such is the boaster's folly. "All such boasting is evil" (v. 16).

Embezzlers of God's Glory. One of the lowest forms of egomania is taking the credit when it belongs to someone else. "Giving credit where credit is due" reflects a basic tenet of proper speech. It also reflects why God views boasting so seriously.

The basic purpose of our existence is to reflect God's glory. God has designed His glory to be reflected through the universe, the Children of Israel, the Word of God, Christ, humanity, and the believer. We glorify God by demonstrating who and what He is through our attitudes and activities. Paul told the believers in Corinth, "Your body is the temple of the Holy Ghost which is in you, which ye have of God, and ye are not your own. For ye are bought with a price; therefore *glorify God* in your body" (1 Cor. 6:19-20, KJV).

I've often wondered about God's denial of Moses' entrance into the Promised Land. Certainly there was more to it than just an angry striking of the rock. Psalm 106:33 says that Moses "spoke unadvisedly with his lips" (KJV). In Numbers 20:7-12, we read that Moses said to the Israelites, "Must *we* bring you water out of this rock?" (v. 10) Moses had taken the honor that belonged to God. It was because he embezzled God's glory that he was not permitted into the Promised Land.

In a study of morality in America, *Psychology Today* found that 95 percent of those they polled felt that "accepting praise for another's work" was unethical (James Hassett, "But That Would Be Wrong," *Psychology Today,* November 1981, p. 34). If our relativistic culture is sensitive to this matter, we can imagine how God must view our accepting the credit for His work in us.

For Herod, accepting the praise of men who acclaimed him as God meant instant death. "Immediately, because Herod did not give praise to God, an angel of the Lord struck him down, and he was eaten by worms and died" (Acts 12:23).

Is it any wonder that when it came to the important process of salvation, God did all the work to make it possible? He knew if we helped save ourselves we'd boast about it. That's why eternal life is "not by works, so that no man can boast" (Eph. 2:9).

In each of these three pictures of boasting, God is eliminated from His rightful place. In the inflation of our nothingness, God's work in us is ignored. When we boast of our abilities to be or to gain, God's divine oversight and control of our lives is overlooked.

It is not surprising that when God's Word lists the characteristics of godless people, boasters often find their places in the list. In Romans 1, boasters are included in the godless company of slanderers, God-haters, the insolent, and arrogant (Rom. 1:30). Paul describes the godless in the last days by saying they will be "lovers of themselves, lovers of money, boastful, proud, abusive, disobedient to their parents, ungrateful, unholy" (2 Tim. 3:2).

"O Lord, the God who avenges, O God who avenges, shine forth. Rise up, O Judge of the earth; pay back to the proud what they deserve. How long will the wicked, O Lord, how long will the wicked be jubilant? They pour out arrogant words; all the evildoers are full of boasting" (Ps. 94:1-4).

If we must boast, God's Word instructs us to boast in God. "I will extol the Lord at all times; His praise will always be on my lips. My soul will boast in the Lord; let the afflicted hear and rejoice. Glorify the Lord with me; let us exalt His name together" (34:1-3). This boasting in the Lord is not only right, but it is also an encouragement to others. Conversely, when we boast about ourselves we hurt those who are not as blessed as we might be.

In my first pastorate, God blessed the work beyond my

expectations. I recall going to pastors' meetings where I would be asked how things were going. In my lack of sensitivity, I would recite the great things that were happening. It wasn't long until I realized that these words brought discouragement to the other pastors' hearts, especially those whose ministries were small, struggling, and often filled with division and hard feelings. I was communicating a boastful spirit even though I sometimes would sanctimoniously give God the credit as a ritualistic "P. S." When the Lord brought this to my attention, I found that I could have a ministry of encouragement to my fellow pastors by "boasting in the Lord." Comments like, "The Lord has proven faithful," and "He's providing wisdom," puts us on common ground. Turning the conversation then to *their* needs provided an opportunity for me to encourage them.

Flattery

The well-worn quip, "Flattery will get you everywhere" is more truth than fiction. There are fewer skills of the tongue that are more manipulative, more ego-serving than the skill of flattery. Flattery is the hypnotic power of the tongue to seduce and to conquer.

Flattery is the act of placing someone in debt to us by verbally commending some action, virtue, or involvement in his life. The commendation may or may not be true. Flattery differs from genuine praise or compliment because of its motive. Flattery is a compliment shared to manipulate another for personal gain.

There are at least four manipulative abilities within the scope of a flatterer's tongue. *Attention* is one of the payoffs of a flattering tongue. If I tell you what a great job you did in the Sunday School discussion, you will pay attention to me. You will smile, look at me, and thank me. Some of us are so starved for that kind of attention that we use flattery to get it.

Solicited compliments are within the scope of a flatterer's power. Few of us would be so forward as to ask someone to compliment our new clothes. But we might flatter other people about their attractive clothes and hope that they return the compliment. Our flattery puts others in debt to our positive comments about them.

The flatterer uses the power of his words to *seduce*. A flattering tongue can hypnotize others into falling for all kinds of schemes. Immoral, unethical, cruel, and damaging partnerships have often been sealed in a flatterer's parlor. Statements like, "You're a beautiful woman. I just love the way you wear your hair," "I know you're smart enough to know a good deal when you see one," and "I wish my husband were as kind and sensitive as you are" are all traps set in the web of a flatterer's tongue. As Samuel Johnson said, "Men are like stone jugs—you may lug them where you like by their ears."

The flatterer also uses his words to *gain favor*. All of us like to be in good favor with others. True favor comes by earning another's respect. Unfortunately, some of us think we can worm our way into other people's favor by flattering them. There are no shortcuts to real respect and solid relationships. In the long run, flattery only damages and spoils the potential of favor and respect.

The sin of flattery is linked with godlessness, faithlessness, oppression, pride, wickedness, and all that is vile. "Help, Lord, for the godly are no more; the faithful have vanished from among men. Everyone lies to his neighbor; their flattering lips speak with deception. May the Lord cut off all flattering lips and every boastful tongue that says, 'We will triumph with our tongues; we own our lips—who is our master?' " (Ps. 12:1-4)

In Psalm 5:9, the word translated *flatter* (NASB) literally means to "make their tongue smooth." Flatterers are slick in their speech. The *New International Version* translates the word *deceive*. Flattery is a smooth and subtle form of deceit. This makes it difficult to discern. The smooth deceit is doubly dangerous because most of us enjoy the flattery.

Psalm 5:9 also states that a flatterer's words cannot be trusted. "There is nothing reliable in what they say" (NASB). Lastly, verse 9 says that the flatters' throats are like open graves.

Flattery is a reflection of a destructive spirit. When we seek to control or use others for our benefit, we begin to destroy them. A flatterer destroys the object of his flattery by placing the potential of pride and the snare of seduction in his path.

The psalmist recognized this danger in verse 8, "O Lord, lead me in Thy righteousness because of my foes; make Thy way straight before me" (NASB). The word *foes* in this verse actually means "those who lie in wait for me." We should heed God's warning, "Whoever flatters his neighbor is spreading a net for his feet" (Prov. 29:5).

This, of course, does not mean that we should never genuinely compliment, encourage, or praise someone who is deserving of or in need of a positive word. The key is the motivation. Why am I complimenting this person? If it truly is an act of love, encouragement, and support with no thought of personal gain—then it is a compliment, not flattery.

Compliments that give God the glory shield others from the traps of pride and seduction. Comments like, "I'm thankful the Lord has given you such a spirit of encouragement," or "God has been good to give me a husband like you," or "The Lord has given you a special ability to minister to me through song," go a long way to take the flattery factor out of our compliments.

Exaggeration

Someone once said, "I don't exaggerate—I just stretch the truth." Exaggeration is nothing more than lying about details to make information more sensational, interesting, or manipulative. From fishermen to politicians, no one is exempt from the ego-serving tendency of the tongue.

This form of lying is prevalent. Some of us exaggerate to catch people's attention. Have you ever been telling a story when you suddenly realized that you were losing your audience's interest? Almost subconsciously, we add a little zip to the drama. What was only a broken toe at first becomes fatal cancer of the foot after several tellings. We all add a little of our own pizzazz until we have made a mountain out of a molehill.

Have you ever exaggerated to manipulate someone into doing what you wanted them to do? "I'll knock your head off if you don't come here," is the manipulative exaggeration of an angry parent. In fact, anger often vents itself in exaggerated expressions to intimidate or humble those we are angry with. I get a chuckle out of King Nebuchadnezzar who, in his great anger against Shadrach, Meshach, and Abednego, commanded that the furnace be turned up seven times hotter (Dan. 3:19). The fire would have been sufficient just the way it was, but in his anger Nebuchadnezzar had an exaggerated response.

Sometimes we exaggerate to feel better about ourselves and to help others feel better about us as well. The fisherman whose largemouth bass was *just* three pounds ends up telling people that it was *at least* three pounds. The businessman who makes $50,000 a year tells his friend that he's making "something under $100,000 a year." Salesmen face a special temptation in this area. How easy it is to exaggerate the claims of a product to close a sale.

I worked for a carpenter one summer. Occasionally, I would

cut a board too short. He would say, "Get the wood stretcher." His point was that wood doesn't stretch. Neither does the truth. Some of us want to make silly putty of the truth by stretching it to our own fancy. The problem is that stretching the truth destroys it.

Exaggeration erodes trust and credibility, two building blocks of successful relationships. It is a violation of God's will for us. Yielding our egos to be used to serve God and others instead of our own interests will produce words that help and heal. Then with the psalmist we can say, "May the words of my mouth and the meditation of my heart be pleasing in Your sight, O Lord, my Rock and my Redeemer" (Ps. 19:14).

5

CROSS WORDS

Murmuring and contentious words

I recall hanging wallpaper in our kitchen one evening. Everything was ready—the tarp, the tools, and the water trough, which was filled and in place on the floor. With my back turned, I heard the swoosh of rushing water. I looked and my worst fears were realized. There stood my youngest son Matthew, one foot in the trough, one foot in spilled water, and two apprehensive eyes glued on me. With irritation oozing out of my words, I shook my head and said, "You klutz."

Immediately he began to cry. "You klutz" had totally devastated his sense of worth and integrity. My words pierced his young spirit like arrows. Two words were all it took. The spilled water was no longer the issue. The issue was now our relationship. It took hugs and reassuring words to convince him that Daddy's words and spirit had been wrong and that I still thought he was the greatest seven-year-old in the whole world.

Verbal pieces of our minds like complaining, screaming, subtle barbs, nagging, criticism, and angry words are all traits of the tongue's ability to cut and destroy. Those piercing tendencies of the tongue are spoken of in Proverbs 12:18, "There is one who speaks rashly like the thrusts of a sword, but the tongue of the wise brings healing" (NASB). The psalmist declares that our tongues can be "sharp swords" and "as sharp as a serpent's" (Pss. 57:4; 140:3).

There are a variety of roots that bear the fruit of the cross words of a murmuring and contentious tongue.

Anger. Anger is like an inner explosion. It needs an outlet. A common escape valve is our tongue. Angry people are quarrels looking for a place to happen.

Irritation. Sharp words come from the irritation that is produced when people come crashing through our well-ordered lives.

Disappointment. If our disappointment in a person or a situation is strong enough, our words will soon reflect it. Broken expectations hurt. Our disappointed spirits show up in our speech.

Impatience. "Antsie" spirits have a tendency to lose patience through their mouths.

Stress. Lives that are in "overload" tend to have shorter verbal fuses than those that live in an organized, relaxed environment.

Insecurity. Insecurity often resorts to sharp, intimidating, critical words in order to develop a sense of strength and security. Unfortunately, cross words only make for weaker relationships and compounded insecurity.

Guilt. When guilty people are confronted with their guilt, they often respond sharply. Retorts like, "Who do you think you are?" or "I suppose you think you're perfect!" are the barbed defense mechanisms spoken by a person with a guilty conscience.

Scripture indicates that these roots surface in our speech in two general ways. One is the verbal sin of *murmuring.* The other is what we will call a *contentious tongue.*

Murmuring

Some time ago while flying home from the East Coast, I was talking with a Christian doctor about his family. All of his children were grown, happily committed to Christ, and serving in their local churches. The doctor was obviously grateful and relieved that his children had gone on in the faith. As a father of three, I was intensely interested in knowing what he felt the secret was to the spiritual success of his children. He explained, "My wife and I covenanted that our children would never hear us complain or criticize the church, church leaders, or another brother or sister in Christ." In essence, he had made a commitment not to murmur.

Murmuring is complaining with a critical spirit that harbors a negative attitude toward the situation or the people involved. It runs the continuum from complaining about the slow driver in front of me to murmuring against the Lord for things He has permitted to come into my life. Murmuring carries the potential for great damage. It is a direct violation of God's will.

My doctor friend had wisely realized that complaining about God's work, God's leaders, and God's people was a direct reflection on the value of God, His plan, and His people. What child wants to commit his life to a system and a people who are the constant object of their parents' complaints? A wise parent teaches the principles of love and prayerful intercession in regard to imperfections around us. Murmuring about the family of God only gives excuses to the future potential of rebellion in a child's heart.

Nowhere in Scripture is murmuring more graphically depicted than in the case of the Children of Israel. In fact, they were denied access to the Promised Land because of their murmuring.

When the people of Israel were poised on the edge of the Promised Land, 12 spies were sent to "case out" the territory.

Ten spies came back and said, " 'We can't attack those people; they are stronger than we are.' And they spread among the Israelites a bad report about the land they had explored. They said, 'The land we explored devours those living in it. All the people we saw there are of great size. . . . We seemed like grasshoppers in our own eyes, and we looked the same to them' " (Num. 13:31-33) . However, Joshua and Caleb, while affirming the details of the account, maintained that God was able to give the people the land.

Several aspects of this situation are instructive about murmuring:

1. Murmuring ignores God's potential. The report of the 10 spies was given from a godless perspective. If God had opened the sea to save them, the heavens to free them, the rocks to water them; if He had defeated mighty armies through the wilderness trek, then certainly He could deal with giants in the land.

2. Murmuring was born in the context of bad reports. Sins of the tongue that spread negative reports (beguilement, gossip, slander, false witness) create the environment in which murmuring can thrive. There will always be some people who wait in the wings to hear negative things so that they can have something to complain about.

3. A murmuring spirit is quick to jump to the wrong conclusion. The grumbling Israelites said, "Why is the Lord bringing us to this land only to let us fall by the sword? Our wives and children will be taken as plunder. Wouldn't it be better for us to go back to Egypt?" (14:3) Actually, nothing could have been farther from the truth. But once our godless grumbling gets rolling, wrong conclusions are easy to sell. Murmuring and beguilement go hand in hand.

4. Bad judgments are spawned in the atmosphere of murmuring. The murmuring Israelites decided it would have been better had they died in Egypt. They began planning to go

back to Egypt and to stone the ones who urged them to stop grumbling and trust in the Lord. Murmuring distorts good judgment.

5. Murmuring leads to self-pity. "If only we had died in Egypt! Or in this desert!" (v. 2) Murmurers often feel very sorry for themselves. Look how we've been mistreated, misused, let down!

6. Murmuring thrives in an atmosphere of fear. Twice Joshua and Caleb exhorted the people not to fear (v. 9). Their fear of odds beyond themselves fanned the sparks of murmuring in their midst. They were in a situation beyond their control. They felt threatened and insecure. They had forgotten God and were afraid.

7. Murmuring left unchecked usually breeds rebellion. Joshua and Caleb urged the murmuring Israelites not to "rebel against the Lord." A critical, grumbling, complaining tongue creates a perfect climate for rebellion. The Israelites were ready to elect new leaders and to stone those who opposed their rebellious plans.

8. The end result of a murmuring spirit is a general atmosphere of dissatisfaction. Discontent is fanned by criticism and complaining. By the end of this episode, Israel was dissatisfied with their God-given lot in life.

"Majority reports" are not always true. If a lot of people are murmuring, that doesn't necessarily reflect accuracy of the information or perspective. We tend to wear fear and insecurity close to the surface. Murmuring has no trouble attracting a crowd.

God's judgment on the Israelites was swift and final. Their murmuring had verbally defamed His presence, power, wisdom, and glory. They would not see the Promised Land, and they would be granted their distorted wish to die in the wilderness.

The New Testament illustrates other situations that

promote murmuring. John 6:41-43 indicates that the Pharisees murmured because of *ignorance* and lack of information. Acts 6:1 demonstrates that murmuring can grow out of an *offense*. The widows of the Grecians were neglected. Because of this, the Grecians murmured in the congregation. First Peter 4:9 shows that a *slothful spirit* is ready ground for a murmuring tongue. Paul says, "Do everything without complaining or arguing, so that you may become blameless and pure, children of God without fault in a crooked and depraved generation, in which you shine like stars in the universe" (Phil. 2:14-15). This exhortation follows Paul's reminder that "it is God who works in you to will and to act according to His good purpose" (v. 13). The presence of God and His power in us is a sufficient resource. It provides the ability to cope without murmuring.

Murmuring is always a godless pastime. It overlooks our potential in God. It refuses to believe that God can conquer any circumstances if He so desires. And it refuses to recognize that God may use negative circumstances to work His best in our lives and demonstrate His glory.

Is it ever right to express dissatisfaction? Yes, as long as our spirit is constructive and our trust is in God to ultimately intervene should He so desire. Three steps help to keep our complaints constructive:

1. Prayer. The psalmist often complained to God about his problems. However, it was with confidence in God's faithfulness, power, and love. In praying we should commit our problems to His care and willingly wait for God to solve them or to direct us to His solution.

2. Take the complaint to someone with the authority to rectify the existing situation. Sharing it with those who are not a part of the solution only stimulates murmuring and makes the problem harder to solve. Assure the one in authority of your loyalty and desire to help. Open your mind to his perspective.

3. Encourage others to take the problem to those in a place of authority before they discuss it with you any further.

The Contentious Tongue

An old-time couple, well up in years, were riding in their horse-drawn wagon one evening. They had experienced a rocky marriage. As the two horses, separated only by the tongue of the wagon, pulled them along in the moonlight, something of the early romance grew in the heart of the wife. Noticing how gracefully and cooperatively the horses drew their wagon, she snuggled up to her husband, took his arm, and remarked about how nicely the horses worked together. The husband, after a second of thought, drawled, "We probably could too if we only had one tongue between us."

Contentious tongues create strife, resentment, and division in any relationship. Biblical references to a contentious tongue largely grow out of a few Hebrew words that share the meaning "to have a cause." Though these words are used of good and constructive causes, they are often used as well to indicate "having a cause" in the context of a negative, vengeful spirit. It is in these cases that the words are translated contention, strife, quarreling, and debating.

God's Word descriptively lists the causes of a contentious tongue. Hatred (Prov. 10:12) and a "hot temper" (15:18) are obvious roots. Proverbs 30:33 colorfully adds anger to the list by saying, "For as churning the milk produces butter, and as twisting the nose produces blood, so stirring up anger produces strife."

Greed is an interesting addition to the list (28:25). People bent on their own gain regardless of the cost in relationships or righteous living stir up dissension. Children who hoard their toys and refuse to share, create a spirit of contention with their peers, to say nothing of the children who grab the toys of others for themselves. Adults simply translate toys into dollars and possessions. Contentious tongues are always found around a greedy heart.

Genesis 13 indicates that contention is bred by close quarters and insufficient supply. "Now Lot, who was moving about with Abram, also had flocks and herds and tents. But the land could not support them while they stayed together, for their possessions were so great that they were not able to stay together. And quarreling arose between Abram's herdsmen and the herdsmen of Lot. . . . So Abram said to Lot, 'Let's not have any quarreling between you and me, or between your herdsmen and mine, for we are brothers' " (Gen. 13:5-8). Though most of us don't fight over pasture land, offices with insufficient supply, homes with insufficient room, and relationships with too much competition are prime targets for contentious tongues.

A desire for position and prestige is good ground for contentious words. This tendency toward "big shotitis" was even present with the 12 disciples. After three years of sitting under Christ's ministry, the disciples were still contending with each other over who would be the greatest in the kingdom (Luke 22:24). In fact, that was the subject of the conversation in the Upper Room the final night before Christ went to the cross. On one other occasion the mother of James and John came to Christ asking that her sons would have the highest positions of prestige in the coming kingdom. When the other 10 heard about it, they were indignant (Matt. 20:20-28).

In Proverbs 23:29-30 we read that those who are given to wine reap strife. Innumerable homes and relationships have replaced joyful words with contentious words because of the problem of alcohol.

Another type of verbal contention is a nagging tongue. "Better to live on a corner of the roof than share a house with a quarrelsome wife" (Prov. 21:9). Later we read, "Better to live in a desert than with a quarrelsome and ill-tempered wife" (v. 19). While it is true that husbands can nag, most wives have particular pressures that make them vulnerable to a quarreling spirit. They are responsible for many details that require the cooperation of others—a tidy house, clothes that look nice, and children that appear relatively clean and well put together. Any failure in these areas is a direct reflection on the wife.

In addition to responsibilities that she has limited control over, a wife, by the nature of her role, is especially vulnerable to hurts and disappointments. She would like her husband to communicate with her and to participate (at least mentally) in her life and interests. She wants him to share her concern for the children's welfare and the spiritual climate of the home. When this expectation isn't realized, nagging becomes one way she can let her needs be known. Fortunately, Scripture does give us other ways to cope with these pressures. But for the wife and mother who has not discovered God's better way, nagging is simply a matter of survival.

The most serious result of a contentious tongue is the division and discord that it creates. A quarreling, bickering, contending tongue divides. To God, unity is very important (John 17:11). Both the church and home are called on to reflect the unity of God's true nature (1 Cor. 12:12-31; Eph. 5:22-33). When contentious words cause divisions in the church and at home, we destroy not only the joy of oneness, but also the reflection of God in our midst.

Contentious words are like a meat cleaver in our relationships. I recall watching a butcher prepare a chicken for selling. His sharp cleaver chopped away with calculated well-timed strokes until the bird lay in a dozen pieces. Contentious words are like that. In Proverbs 6:14 and 19 the word for contention is translated "discord" (KJV). "He that soweth discord among the brethren" (v. 19, KJV) makes the infamous list of "six things doth the Lord hate, yea, seven" that are an abomination to the Lord (v. 16, KJV).

In 1 Corinthians 3:3, Paul faults the Corinthians for being contentious with each other. Later on, he pictures the church as the body of Christ working as one in cooperative harmony (12:12-31). Have you ever seen a body cut into several parts functioning well? Division among the brethren destroys the reflection of God through us.

On the home front, our relationship with our spouse is God's living illustration of Christ and the church. Christ never divides Himself from His bride, the church. His unconditional love and acceptance are unifying factors. His words to the church promote healing and growth. When contentious words divide our spirits at home, we destroy the God-intended picture of Christ and His church.

The phrase "divide and conquer" has spiritual validity. Division among God's people gives Satan a tremendous advantage in conquering our usefulness, joy, and peace. The destructive influence of murmuring, contentious words must be exchanged for words that produce confidence in Christ and encouragement to His people. As Paul says, "Do not let any unwholesome talk come out of your mouths, but only what is helpful for building others up according to their needs, that it may benefit those who listen" (Eph. 4:29).

6

EXPLETIVES DELETED

Using God's name in vain and sensuous speech

The official transcript of the Watergate tapes of the Nixon era were frequently interrupted by the phrase, "Expletives deleted." "Expletives deleted" soon became a common term to refer to less than the best of speech. Deleting the expletives indicated that on the level of presidential prestige, *expletives* were an unfitting reflection of the president's character.

Like many standards of society, the decency of a matter is not absolute, but relative. It's interesting that expletives, though unpresidential, are an acceptable part of media entertainment. Some, who are in the business of managing and motivating people, claim that expletives communicate the seriousness of a matter. To them, an appropriate expletive shows that you mean business. But unlike our cultural perceptions, God's Word establishes absolute parameters for our speech.

Using God's Name in Vain

Thou shalt not is God's perspective on using His name in vain (Ex. 20:7, KJV). He not only includes this prohibition in the Ten Commandments, but He also warns that He "will not hold anyone guiltless who misuses His name" (v. 7). Of all the Ten Commandments, this is the only one that receives this stern emphasis.

Taking God's name in vain literally means to use it for that which is "waste and in disorder; hence that which is empty, vain . . . for which there is no occasion" (Keil and Deilitzsh, *Commentaries on the Old Testament*, "The Pentateuch" Vol. II, Eerdmans, p. 118). Essentially, to take God's name in vain means to use it as though it has no worth or value.

Perhaps that's the root of our problem in this area—we don't appreciate the real value of God's name. Too often we interpret God from our limited point of view instead of letting God interpret His worth and value from His point of view. Perceiving God in our own image leads to distortion and idolatry.

Looking at God's name from a cultural point of view distorts our sense of its worth and dulls our sensitivity to its proper use. Culturally, names are merely cosmetic. When a child is born, a name is often chosen because it sounds pleasant. For most of us, names have no intrinsic value.

But with God's name it is different. God's name has value and worth. The significance of God's name must be grasped in two dimensions: its significance to God and its experiential significance to us.

Significance to God. God's name is a revelation of His glory. It is the communication of His character. It is intrinsically tied to His being.

When Moses asked the voice in the burning bush, "Suppose I go to the Israelites and say to them, 'The God of your fathers has sent me to you,' and they ask me, 'What is His name?' Then what shall I tell them?" God said to Moses, "I am who I am. This is what you are to say to the Israelites: 'I AM has sent me to you.' " God also said to Moses, "Say to the Israelites, 'The Lord, the God of your fathers—the God of Abraham, the God of Isaac and the God of Jacob—has sent me to you.' This is My name forever, the name by which I am to be remembered from generation to generation" (Ex. 3:13-15). God's name revealed that He was the eternally self-existent One, personally identified with Israel through the patriarchs.

Throughout the Old Testament, God's names reveal detailed aspects of His glory. Even the word *name,* used in reference to God, became an all inclusive statement for the revelation of all that God is. The psalmist said, "I will declare Thy name" (Ps. 22:22, KJV). In other words, I will speak about all that You are. When Isaiah warned that the "name of the Lord" was coming, he meant that God was coming in all of His justice, wrath, and holiness (Isa. 30:27). The Old Testament claims, "The *name* of the Lord is a strong tower, the righteous run into it and are safe" (Prov. 18:10). David writes that God's name will endure forever (Ps. 72:17). An awareness of these realities helps us develop a true sense of the dignity, worth, and value that belongs to God's name. His name is the vehicle of the revelation of His glory to mankind.

This is also demonstrated in the names of Christ. His names are revelatory of His character, worth, and work. The name *Christ* is the title of His Messiahship. It communicates that He is the promised King. It reflects the integrity of God in keeping His promise to Israel. *Immanuel* means "God with us" (Matt. 1:23). The name *Jesus* was especially prescribed by the angel because it is the word for Saviour. "He will save His people from their sins" (v. 21).

The name of Jesus carries power over evil spirits (7:22) and power in prayer (John 14:13-14). It is the authority by which the Holy Spirit comes (v. 26). It is the authority for salvation (Rom. 10:13) and baptism (Matt. 28:19-20).

The name of Jesus is important to God. Paul writes,

"Therefore God exalted Him to the highest place and gave Him the name that is above every name, that at the name of Jesus every knee should bow, in heaven and on earth and under the earth, and every tongue confess that Jesus Christ is Lord, to the glory of God the Father" (Phil. 2:9-11). God guarantees that *every tongue* will bow to Jesus' name. It is a submission to all Christ claims to be. All those who have made an expletive of His name will one day exalt Him.

Likewise, the Father's name is important to Christ. When Jesus taught the disciples to pray, He said, "Our Father in heaven, hallowed be Your name" (Matt. 6:9). The word *hallowed* literally means sacred, set apart, holy. Christ's petition at the opening of His prayer was that the Father's name would be honored and revered. The sacredness of the Father's name was a priority concern of the Saviour.

Old Testament Jews so reverenced the name of Jehovah that they took away its vowels when they wrote it so that it could not be spoken, only symbolized. Tradition says that at one point in their history, the Jews refused to use God's name in a conversation with a non-Jew.

In the Old Testament we are instructed to love, wait on, bless, praise, walk in, think on, and fear God's name (Pss. 5:11; 52:9; 145:1-2; Joel 2:26; Micah 4:5; Mal. 3:16; 4:2). All of this shows that God's name is important to Him. Theologically speaking, His names are not adjectives—they are nouns. His names are more than descriptive, they are substantive.

Taking God's name in vain indicates our religious temperature. When we use one of His names in an empty, negative context, it demonstrates His true worth in our estimation. It is the ultimate statement of a wicked and proud heart to callously degrade God's name.

Significance to us. Names gain value and worth by experience. My wife may think that Amy is the cutest name for a baby girl, but I may remember an Amy who always refused to go out with me on dates. If Sam was the name of the bully on my wife's block, regardless of how appropriate I may think the name is, it will never be the name of my son.

When I was in high school, the greatest insult you could hurl at another guy was to use his mother's name in some crude context. "Mother" meant something special; it represented worth and value. It was a violation of both heart and mind to hear it used wrongly.

The names of those we love are precious to us. It should concern us to hear anyone, especially believers, use God's name in calloused, casual, and flippant ways. Expressions such as "Oh, God," "God," and "My Lord" are often used as verbal exclamation points. Jokes that make light of His value and sacred worth are woven into the social fare of some Christian gatherings. Even expressions like "Praise the Lord" are thrown around with such frequency that they become empty religious phrases.

As we grow in the Lord, He becomes more precious to us. As we experience the depth of His saving work, the name *Jesus* becomes one that we love. As we realize the joy of submitting to His sovereign authority, the name *Lord* becomes precious to us. An increasing awareness of all that God is elevates the name of God in our hearts. We honor and revere it with our tongues.

Sensuous Speech

Expressions of immoral, sensual speech are not compatible with our newness in Christ. Words, phrases, stories, jokes, and tales that deal with immorality are clearly renounced in Scripture.

> But among you there must not be even a hint of sexual immorality, or any kind of impurity, or of greed, because these are improper for God's holy people. Nor should there be obscenity, foolish talk or coarse joking, which

are out of place, but rather thanksgiving. For of this you can be sure: No immoral, impure or greedy person—such a man is an idolater—has any inheritance in the kingdom of Christ and of God. Let no one deceive you with empty words, for because of such things God's wrath comes on those who are disobedient. Therefore do not be partners with them. For you were once darkness, but now you are light in the Lord. Live as children of light (for the fruit of the light consists in all goodness, righteousness and truth) and find out what pleases the Lord. Have nothing to do with the fruitless deeds of darkness, but rather expose them. For it is shameful even to mention what the disobedient do in secret (Eph. 5:3-12).

Our increased openness to immoral speech is a reflection not only of the nature of our flesh, but also of the tremendous amount of immoral input from our culture. With our sophisticated media capacities to produce, reproduce, and communicate, it is not surprising that these capabilities are being used to feed our passions.

Twenty-four hours a day we can feed our lusts. From soft and hard pornography, to movies, to home movie hookups, to videotapes, to soap operas, to prime time television—the input is everywhere, both in overt and subtle ways. Even advertising is often based on sensual innuendos, if not outright seduction. Many styles of dress both for men and women feature the shallow appeal of sensuous signals. With all of this input, sensual output is a predictable result.

As Christians, our sensitivities have been dulled. What would have raised red flags just a few years ago now raises smiles and rapt attention with little twinge of conscience. Marginal expressions, questionable jokes, words and phrases with double meanings are tolerated and often enjoyed. This, unfortunately, leads to a greater openness to the sins of the flesh. Some believers openly attend movies that are laced with violence, obscene language, and sexual experiences graphically portrayed.

It seems that television has been the most influential instrument in lulling Christians to sleep about decency and purity. While speaking at a deacons' retreat of a solid biblically based church, I noticed that several made a quick exodus from the dinner table Friday night. They were excitedly talking about getting back to their rooms so that they wouldn't miss the next episode of "Dallas." As you probably know, "Dallas" is rated as one of the loosest serials on prime-time television. Its plot is woven with adultery, unfaithfulness, greed, and violence.

To me, that was symptomatic. It said something about our sensitivity to moral purity. How many Christian housewives are hooked on afternoon "soaps," where there is now more explicit sex per hour than on prime-time evening television? Perhaps we have deceived ourselves into thinking that we can be observers without it affecting our talk and our lifestyle. We are becoming dangerously open to the input of immorality and ungodliness. Tragically, this input soon shows up in output. As they say in computer programming, "Garbage in, garbage out."

Guidelines for Pure Speech

God draws a clear, unmoving line in the sand of the moral desert of our day. To the Ephesians, who lived in an immoral culture, Paul said that immorality should not even be hinted at among believers (Eph. 5:3), literally, "not even mentioned." Paul lists obscenity, foolish talk, and coarse joking as things we should avoid (v. 4). Obscenity literally means anything that is opposed to purity or morality. Its antonym in the Greek means that which is good, moral, or beautiful. Words, expressions, stories, and conversations that oppose

God's standards of purity and morality are out-of-bounds. Our newness in Christ demands clean, moral, and beautiful words.

Foolish talk is described by one Greek scholar as talk that is offensive to Christian decency. This would certainly include words that are vulgar and indecent in their connotations. Speech that is from a foolish heart is godless speech. Since God is pleased with modesty (1 Tim. 2:9), then talk that makes light of modesty and condones immodesty is foolish. Since God is concerned about loyalty in marriage, then words that make light of marital fidelity are foolish as well.

Coarse joking is the translation of a Greek word that literally means "that which turns easily." It is the lighthearted, sinful speech that is full of double meanings—jokes, puns, and even plays-on-words. Advertising, television dramas, and general conversation abound with this sin of the tongue. It is so engrained in us that it takes diligence to avoid the turning of our tongues.

In Ephesians 5 there are two levels of appeal to reflect morality in speech. The first is our *holy standing* before God (Eph. 5:3). We have been made righteous in Christ at salvation. We are a holy priesthood (1 Peter 2:5). The goal of growing believers is to match our living with our standing before God. The second level of appeal is simple *decency*. Crude talk is "out of place" for the Christian (Eph. 5:4).

Warnings about Sensual Speech

First, Paul warns us to beware of those who would deceive us with empty words (Eph. 5:6). This verse infers that the deceit is in reference to God's view of immoral behavior and immoral speech. The truth is that God's wrath comes on this kind of disobedience.

Some people try to deceive us into thinking that those who

adhere to God's moral standards are legalists. Being "up-to-date," "open-minded," or "able to deal with" sinful input are all rationalizations that appeal to our pride. God's Word says, "Do not be deceived: God cannot be mocked. A man reaps what he sows" (Gal. 6:7).

Second, God warns us against partnership with moral decadence (Eph. 5:7). Verbal, visual, and economic partnerships are easily struck with impurity in our "no holds barred" society. But believers must refuse to be friends with the world system (James 4:4).

Third, we must remember that we are children of the light (Eph. 5:8-14). We are no longer a part of the darkness. When we revert to our old patterns and walk in darkness, we break our fellowship with God and violate His will for us (1 John 1:5-7; 2 Cor. 6:14—7:1).

Practically speaking, sensuous speech:

- neutralizes our sensitivity to moral purity
- contributes to a sensual mind set
- reflects a lack of self-control
- seduces people into believing that we're sexually vulnerable
- robs God of His glory in our speech

Paul gives two suggestions for transforming our sensuous speech patterns. We should speak words that are "helpful for building others up according to their needs, that it may benefit those who listen" (Eph. 4:29). Sensuous speech obviously hinders. Instead of building up, it tears down. It weakens our resistance to immorality. It does not benefit those who listen. A commitment to words that build and benefit will eliminate sensuous speech.

We are also to enjoy the verbal pleasures of sharing grateful words with each other (5:4). Immorality breeds discontent. Feeding our lusts verbally and visually develops an ungratefulness for what we presently have sexually. It leads our discontent on an insatiable journey through a maze of sexual fantasies and experiments—always searching for, yet never finding, the ultimate experience.

On the other hand, purity leaves our lives uncluttered, free to know, experience, and proclaim God's greatness. Helpful, constructive, beneficial words—words that reflect the joy of thanksgiving and praise—are spoken by a truly transformed tongue.

Tongues that honor God's name and reflect purity are of value to God and others. As our words transcribe themselves into people's lives, may they note that the expletives have been deleted.

7

HEART TALK

Your tongue reflects your spirit

When it comes to a dandelion, the key to its survival is its root. Children pick bouquets of them, but as long as their roots remain they'll keep growing back. Part of my responsibility as a boy was to dig the dandelions out of our lawn. My dad always said, "Be sure to get the root."

The problem of dandelions and the problem of our tongues have one thing in common—roots. Those of us who try to solve sinful speech patterns from the neck up find that the problems keep coming back. But our speech problems are really heart problems, for our tongues are in reality the servants of our spirits. The root of my talk is the condition of my heart. Our tongues simply reveal what's happening inside of us.

Before we were married, my wife and I would often double-date with friends. On one such occasion while driving home from a basketball game, Martie and I heard soft singing coming from the backseat. My friend was the star, All-American pitcher for our college baseball team. His date was one of the prettiest girls on campus. Yet this macho athlete was actually serenading his fiancee. Though it wasn't the average approach to courtship, he had a heart "condition" that needed to be expressed.

All talk is really heart talk. Granted, some people seem to talk from the neck up. Empty flattery, heartless sermons, ritual responses, and hymns sung without meaning are all shallow utterances. But even these reflect an insincere heart.

Christ recognized that all talk is heart talk when He said, "Make a tree good and its fruit will be good, or make a tree bad and its fruit will be bad, for a tree is recognized by its fruit. You brood of vipers, how can you who are evil say anything good? For out of the overflow of the heart the mouth speaks. The good man brings good things out of the good stored up in him, and the evil man brings evil things out of the evil stored up in him. But I tell you that men will have to give account on the day of judgment for every careless word they have spoken. For by your words you will be acquitted, and by your words you will be condemned" (Matt. 12:33-37).

At this juncture in Christ's ministry the Pharisees had explained the miracles of Christ by saying that "it is only by Beelzebub, the prince of demons, that this fellow drives out demons" (v. 24). Christ responded by affirming that what they had said was a reflection of their wicked hearts.

In fact, our words are such an accurate reflection of our spiritual condition that Christ concludes this section by saying that our words will be the basis for His judgment. We will be held accountable for our words, not because God is a "nit-picker," but because our words are the affirmation of our true inner condition.

Paul reflects on heart talk when he writes, "There is no one righteous, not even one; there is no one who understands, no one who seeks God. All have turned away, they have together become worthless; there is no one who does good, not even one. Their throats are open graves; their tongues practice deceit. The poison of vipers is on their lips. Their mouths are full of cursing and bitterness. Their feet are swift to shed blood; ruin and misery mark their ways, and the way of peace they do not know. There is no fear of God before their eyes" (Rom. 3:10-18).

Notice that after a general description of the Romans' spiritual disability (vv. 10-12), Paul specifically details the tongue as the initial manifestation of their inner worthlessness (vv. 13-14). I am struck by the emphasis on the tongue in this passage. Of all the ways in which we ventilate inner wickedness, the tongue receives priority attention.

A sinful heart produces sinful speech. The picture here is vivid: their throats are like open graves. Open graves vent the smell of death. Our throats, tongues, and lips are all a part of the ventilation of our inner spiritual condition.

My friends in medicine tell me that certain sicknesses produce terrible breath odors. So it is with sin. It is vented through the mouth, disseminated by the tongue, and its deadly potential waits in the lips.

I remember one day at kindergarten when I spouted off at my teacher. I can't recall what stimulated the crisis, but I told my teacher to shut up. Then I stood up, left the room, and started to walk home. As I walked down the block, I noticed that my mother was working in the backyard. I stopped dead in my tracks. What would I tell her?

My options sped before me—face my mother, face the teacher, or walk alone into the big cruel world. I chose the least of the three evils and went back to school. My teacher met me at the door, took me by the arm, and marched me to the restroom where she washed my mouth out with soap.

It was a great lesson. But to be honest, I needed more than a mouthwash. I needed a heart wash. My little five-year-old spirit had shown up in my mouth.

James refers to the tongue as a "bit," a "rudder," and a "fire" (James 3:3-6). All of these commodities are secondary to primary causes. The horse's bit is controlled by the rider, the rudder is wielded by the helmsman, and the fire is born in the spark. So our tongues march to the drumbeat of our spirits.

The fact that our tongues reveal our inner selves can be embarrassing. It's like our slip showing below the hemline of our well-dressed lives. We get all polished up, but then we open our mouths and our spirit shows. Some of us don't even know it! If we knew it, perhaps we'd do something about it. But then, what could we do?

We could stop talking. "Even a fool is thought wise if he keeps silent, and discerning if he holds his tongue" (Prov. 17:28). But we can't keep quiet forever.

Holding our tongues is like having our jaws wired shut to lose weight. It may be a temporary fix, but as soon as we unwire them, if we haven't changed our eating habits, the weight will return. Weight loss needs more than a shut mouth; it needs inner change. It's that way with our speech. Though silence is golden, it is not the key to a transformed tongue.

A businessman approached me after an evening service recently and told me how frustrated he had been by trying to control his speech. Repeated commitments and gimmicks had only ended in repeated failure. That evening we discussed the biblical truth that our tongues are the servants of our spirits. He left with a new resolve to get right to the heart of the matter.

In nearly every Scripture passage where the tongue is mentioned or illustrated, there is a corollary revelation of the heart problem that prompted the sinful talk. Surveying these heart problems is step one in transforming our speech from the inside out. Though often escaping iron-clad classifications, our sins of the tongue are caused by the heart sins of pride, anger, and fear.

The Proud Heart

Spiritually speaking, pride is the elevation of self at the expense of God and His glory. It results in a self-serving lifestyle. Pride has no place for God. It takes credit for what God has done and given. "In his pride the wicked does not seek Him; in all his thoughts there is no room for God" (Ps. 10:4).

Pride is directly connected with negative speech patterns in a variety of ways. Proverbs 8:13 states that pride and arrogance result in evil behavior and perverse speech. Psalm 10 attributes boasting, reviling the Lord, cursing, lying, and contention to pride. Flattery is linked to a boasting spirit in Psalm 12. Psalm 59 indicates that those who are proud slander the righteous. Gossip is another product of a proud heart. Those who gossip are described as insolent and arrogant (Rom. 1:29-30). Scoffing, malice, and oppressive threats are catalogued with a proud spirit (Ps. 73:6-11).

Pride also breeds quarrels (Prov. 13:10). When Hannah was found barren, Elkanah's other wife often taunted her verbally. "And because the Lord had closed her womb, her rival kept provoking her in order to irritate her. This went on year after year. Whenever Hannah went up to the house of the Lord, her rival provoked her till she wept and would not eat" (1 Sam. 1:6-7). Then, when Hannah bore Samuel, she prayed a prayer of thanksgiving in which she recognized that the cruel words of her rival were from a proud spirit. She prayed, "Do not keep talking so proudly or let your mouth speak such arrogance, for the Lord is a God who knows, and by Him deeds are weighed" (2:3).

The Old Testament concept of a fool parallels the essence of a proud spirit. "The fool hath said in his heart, 'There is no God'" (Pss. 14:1, 53:1, KJV). From the foolish heart come slander, promotion of careless opinions, perversion, quarreling, and angry words (Prov. 10:18; 18:2; 19:1; 20:3; 29:11). Is it any wonder that "the mouth of a fool invites ruin"? (10:14)

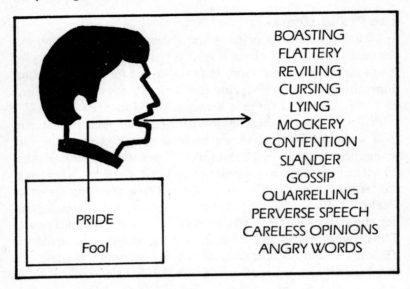

BOASTING
FLATTERY
REVILING
CURSING
LYING
MOCKERY
CONTENTION
SLANDER
GOSSIP
QUARRELLING
PERVERSE SPEECH
CARELESS OPINIONS
ANGRY WORDS

PRIDE

Fool

The Angry Heart

Anger is one of our most powerful emotions. It has the capacity for destruction on both the personal and social levels. Though it is vented in many ways, it is often expressed through our words. Hatred and bitterness are the bedfellows of unresolved anger. They are the poison fruit of long-term anger.

Dissension, lying lips, strife, and threats are all tagged as the tongue's response to an angry spirit (Prov. 10:12,18; 15:18; 24:28-29; 29:22; 30:33). Slander, murmuring, and cruel words are obvious outgrowths of an angry heart (Deut. 1; Num. 14; Prov. 27:4).

Israel became angry with the Lord when the 10 spies returned with the fearful and godless report about Canaan. This anger, mixed with fear and disappointment, led to rebellious words. They said to each other, "We should choose a leader and go back to Egypt" (Num. 14:4). Rebellion, both in spirit and in word, is often the result of anger. Children may let their anger toward their parents issue in a rebellious spirit and rebellious words. That's exactly why God cautioned parents not to provoke their children to anger (Eph. 6:4). It makes them vulnerable to rebellion.

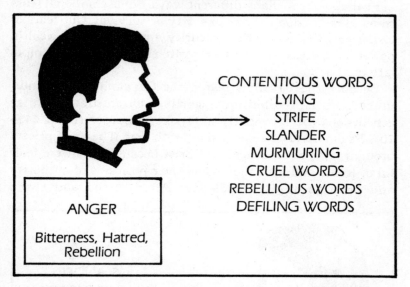

CONTENTIOUS WORDS
LYING
STRIFE
SLANDER
MURMURING
CRUEL WORDS
REBELLIOUS WORDS
DEFILING WORDS

ANGER

Bitterness, Hatred, Rebellion

The same is true in any authority-submission relationship. Anger toward an authority is quickly turned to rebellion, which is conveniently vented through our speech. Anyone in authority who notices disloyal chatter among his subordinates should check and see if he has in some way caused them to be angry.

"See to it that no one misses the grace of God and that no bitter root grows up to cause trouble and defile many" (Heb. 12:15). This verse makes it clear that a bitter spirit has the great potential of trouble and defilement. Many are defiled through the words of a bitter heart.

The Fearful Heart

When Franklin D. Roosevelt said, "We have nothing to fear but fear itself," he said a mouthful. Fear has a great ability to manipulate not only our tongues, but entire nations, races, and cultures.

Fear appears in many different ways. Some emotional fears come from sudden threats to safety or survival. Our fears of losing position, reputation, security, family, friends, wealth, power, happiness, or future gain often motivate and manipulate us.

Because the Israelites feared the Canaanites, they murmured, spread rebellious words, communicated false conclusions (beguilement), and spoke of murder (Num. 14:9-10). Psalm 31:11-13 relates slander to fear. The chief priests brought false witness against Christ because they were fearful of Rome and fearful of losing their positions of authority and prestige (Matt. 26:59-61). Peter cursed and swore

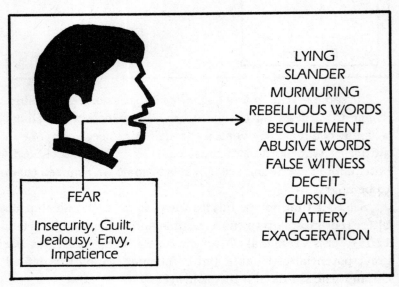

FEAR

Insecurity, Guilt, Jealousy, Envy, Impatience

LYING
SLANDER
MURMURING
REBELLIOUS WORDS
BEGUILEMENT
ABUSIVE WORDS
FALSE WITNESS
DECEIT
CURSING
FLATTERY
EXAGGERATION

because he feared being discovered as one of Christ's disciples (vv. 73-74). The Pharisees lied to protect their position when they were fearful of a national acceptance of Christ as the Messiah (John 8:44-45).

Sometimes we threaten others with abusive speech because they make us feel fearful and insecure. Fear of "getting caught" can lead to deceit, if not outright lying. Fear of loss of friendship or attention could lead to flattery and exaggeration.

Granted, certain fears and insecurities are often used by God to produce growth and discipline. Unfortunately, many do not yield their fears to God. As a result, they spin out on a self-oriented "survival track" that leads to frantic and destructive responses. It's no secret that these fearful responses often show up in our speech.

A New Heart

When Dr. Christian Barnard pioneered the first heart transplant surgery, there was great hope for those with heart trouble. Though the technique of physical heart transplants is still being refined, spiritual heart transplants are readily available.

As for King Saul, "God gave him another heart" (1 Sam. 10:9, KJV), that he might have the ability to exercise the duties of a king. David saw that God could transform us within when he prayed, "Create in me a clean heart, O God; and renew a right spirit within me" (Ps. 51:10, KJV). "If anyone is in Christ, he is a new creation; the old has gone, the new has come!" (2 Cor. 5:17)

Expelling the verbal villains of pride, anger, and fear will not be easy. They are Satan's stranglehold on our spiritual potential for growth and effectiveness. But God can plant genuine humility in the place of pride, patience in the place of anger, and love in the place of fear. Humility, patience, and love reigning in our hearts will stimulate words that are pleasing to God and helpful to those around us.

8

SPEAKING OUT FOR #1

Push your pride aside

The other morning while standing in line at my favorite donut shop, the man who came in after me called out to the approaching clerk, "One small coffee, black." I was incensed. I was next and he knew it. I decided not to make an issue out of it and quietly muttered, "I was next" to the clerk. I thought, *This guy is really rude.* But then, as I fussed over it, I realized that he was simply someone who had subscribed to the ethic of our culture.

"Looking out for #1" has become the main goal of the truly modern person. Self-fulfillment, self-elevation, and self-advancement are priority standards of behavior. In essence, though couched in modern terms and well-spun philosophies, these principles are nothing more than a restatement of pride. It is pride coming out of the closet—parading itself as the truly successful way to live.

At its very core, pride wants to make *self* the most important person in the universe. When Satan was judged by God, he was judged for pride. Satan said in his heart, "I will ascend to heaven; I will raise my throne above the stars of God; I will sit enthroned on the mount of assembly, on the utmost heights of the sacred mountain. I will ascend above the tops of the clouds; I will make myself like the Most High" (Isa. 14:13-14). He wanted to be number one.

Pride strikes a friendship with God only when it is convenient; it establishes friendships that promote itself; it takes orders only from within, and it seeks the accumulation of wealth, status, fame, and glory. Pride seeks to control at any cost and to accomplish its own end regardless of the price.

Proud hearts are guilty of many sins of the tongue. A proud spirit is one that boasts, flatters, reviles, curses, lies, mocks, slanders, gossips, and quarrels. A proud heart is also quick to grow angry and to use careless words. To remedy these patterns, the proud spirit must be transformed.

The Answer to Pride

Pride often reigns within us in subtle ways. People who do not *appear* arrogant and haughty can still possess spirits of pride. Sometimes people who hold high positions of spiritual influence are bound by pride. Often Christians who outwardly conform to lists of standards are proud of their "righteous" living. Other Christians, who feel they are more mature in their freedom than the "legalists," often exhibit pride by assuming a spirit of superiority.

Quiet, unassuming individuals may sometimes appear to be truly humble—when in reality they may feel intimidated and fiercely jealous of others. Counterfeit humility is usually present in the "I am nothing" kind of spirit. Ironically, falsely humble individuals are often proud of their self-assigned humility.

In our battle against pride, some of us fail to get victory because we dwell on expelling what is wrong without replacing it with what is right. Implementing the principles of the new nature permits God's power to chase the villains of the flesh out of our lives.

Love dispels self-centeredness. Those who serve money begin to use their money to serve God. Angry hearts apply the new nature skills of patience. But as soon as we stop the implementation of these skills of the Spirit, the villains of the flesh come back.

Paul wrote, "I have been crucified with Christ and I no longer live, but Christ lives in me. The life I live in the body, I live by faith in the Son of God, who loved me and gave Himself for me" (Gal. 2:20). True humility is the quality of the new nature that replaces a heart of pride. There are two basic ingredients that replace pride with true humility.

The first ingredient replaces the pride of assuming that *I* am the final authority in my life. Pride resists the reality of God's right to unconditionally call the shots in my life. It urges me to assume the role of master. But God is the sovereign Ruler of all creation. He is Lord. *The humble spirit gladly submits to God's rightful place.*

The second ingredient replaces the pride of assuming that *I* am responsible for my own good fortune. Pride urges me to claim the credit for myself. But God's Word teaches that my position, wealth, health, goods, and abilities are ultimately gifts from God. *Humility gives credit where credit is due.* It gladly claims that I am what I am by God's grace and that apart from Him I would be nothing.

Putting God In His Place

Humility submits to God's right to unquestionably rule my life. This is pointedly portrayed in Moses' approach to Pharaoh when God accused Pharaoh of a lack of humility in resisting His Word. Moses confronted Pharaoh and said, "This is what the Lord, the God of the Hebrews, says: 'How long will you refuse to humble yourself before Me? Let My people go, so that they may worship Me' " (Ex. 10:3). The same thrust is given in 1 Peter 5:6 where we are commanded, "Humble yourselves, therefore, under God's mighty hand." God is the ultimate point of authority in the universe. A humble spirit submits to that.

Humility puts God in His place. In reality, He is Number One. The truly humble person has discovered that. The measure of your humility can be determined by God's place in your life.

This distinctive of humility then can be very assertive, bold, and courageous. It develops a tenacious loyalty and an undaunted strength to serve God. It will show in my speech. A heart that is yielded to God will eliminate rebellious, murmuring, angry, lying, and slanderous words. In fact, if Christ is Lord then every sin of the tongue becomes distasteful to me. A spirit that has put God in His rightful place will:

- reject unrighteous suggestions and claims
- express loyalty to God's will regardless of the cost
- worship and praise God for who He is, not just for what He has done
- speak God's truth in the face of rebellion and error
- encourage others to yield to God's rightful place

Putting God in His place allows us to relate properly to each other. As we humbly submit to God, He then asks us to submit to one another (John 13:34-35; Eph. 5:21). Humility is not simply a vertical response—it is horizontal as well.

As we submit to the Lord, then we must submit to one another (Eph. 5:21); to the needs of our wives (Eph. 5:25-33); to the headship of our husbands (Eph. 5:22-24); to the needs of our children (Eph. 6:4); to our parents (Eph. 6:1); younger men to older men (1 Peter 5:5); to the Word of God (John 14:21); to spiritual leaders (Heb. 13:17); to government authority (Rom. 13:1); and to the needs of others in general and especially to the needs of our brothers and sisters in Christ (Gal. 6:10).

Paul wrote, "Do nothing out of selfish ambition or vain conceit, but in humility consider others better than yourselves. Each of you should look not only to your own interests, but also to the interests of others. Your attitude should be the same as that of Christ Jesus: who, being in very nature God, did not consider equality with God something to be grasped, but made Himself nothing, taking the very nature of a servant, being made in human likeness. And being found in appearance as a man, He humbled Himself and became obedient to death—even death on a cross!" (Phil. 2:3-8)

As we yield to God in relationship to others, our words will reflect that as well. Speech patterns that destroy others—such as beguilement, gossip, slander, flattery, contentious words, false witness, and sensuous speech—will give way to words that:

- speak to the needs and interests of others
- protect people from damage
- express genuine concern for others
- communicate comfort, love, joy, understanding, encouragement, and peace
- carefully build up others in spirit and mind
- encourage positive thoughts toward God, self, and others
- promote pure thoughts and right relationships

The God-Made Man

We hear a lot about the self-made man. A part of the American dream is the ability to pull ourselves up by our own boot straps. Though not consciously intended to preclude God from His place as ultimate provider, these ideas focus on our abilities to be self-sufficient.

While it is true that God has chosen to use human instrumentality, He remains the primary and ultimate source of all that we have and are. In Scripture God often proved Himself as the ultimate source. This was such an important lesson for Israel to learn that He gave them daily demonstrations.

> In the wilderness He fed you manna which your fathers did not know, that He might humble you and that He might test you, to do good for you in the end. Otherwise you may say in your heart, 'My power and the strength of my hand made me this wealth.' But you shall remember the Lord your God, for it is He who is giving you power to make wealth, that He may confirm His covenant which He swore to your fathers, as it is this day" (Deut. 8:16-18, NASB).

Before the manna came, Israel hungered (v. 3). God brought them to the end of themselves. Then, in the provision of manna, He daily demonstrated that He is the primary source of provision and life. The lesson of this humbling was "to teach you that man does not live on bread alone, but by every word that comes from the mouth of the Lord. Your clothes did not wear out and your feet did not swell during these forty years" (vv. 3-4).

Earlier God had forged this concept into their minds when He said, "When the Lord your God brings you into the land He swore to your fathers, to Abraham, Isaac and Jacob, to give you—a land with large, flourishing cities *you did not build,* houses filled with all kinds of good things *you did not provide,* wells *you did not dig,* and vineyards and olive groves *you did not plant*—then when you eat and are satisfied, be careful that you do not forget the Lord, who brought you out of Egypt, out of the land of slavery" (Deut. 6:10-12).

God knows that self-sufficiency breeds pride. He also knows that God-sufficiency—knowing that I am what I am and have what I have because of Him—breeds a grateful worshiping spirit.

Success sometimes goes to a person's head. When we forget that what we are and have is because of God, then we become spoiled with pride. We think more of ourselves than we ought, we cease to be grateful to God, and we claim the glory that belongs to Him. God was jealous that the abundant provision of the Promised Land wouldn't go to the Israelites' heads.

On occasion, God permits suffering instead of success. Humility demands that we submit to God's provision in bad times as well as good. A proud spirit shakes its fist in God's face. Pride is unwilling to accept growth and glory through pressure and pain. It demands life on its own terms. The counsel of Job's wife, "Curse God and die!" was the result of a proud spirit (Job 2:9). Job's reply, "Though He slay me, yet will I trust in Him" (13:15, KJV), reflected the courageous strength of humility.

Paul reflected the same humility under pressure when he wrote, "Three times I pleaded with the Lord to take it away from me. But He said to me, 'My grace is sufficient for you, for My power is made perfect in weakness.' Therefore I will boast all the more gladly about my weaknesses, so that Christ's power may rest on me. That is why, for Christ's sake, I delight in weaknesses, in insults, in hardships, in persecutions, in difficulties. For when I am weak, then I am strong" (2 Cor. 12:8-10).

It is important to God that our spirits are gratefully humble toward His design and supply in our lives—whether it be easy street or a trial under which we are assigned to live. In fact, as it was with Israel's hunger and manna, God will often humble us through trials to prepare us to have a grateful spirit of humility in the good times that are to come.

Upon going to our first pastorate, the small group of believers in the church made a great financial commitment to insure that I could be involved in the ministry full time. It was a big step of faith for them. What they didn't know was that it meant a 33 percent cut in income for our family. Those were the manna years of our living. Our whole family learned that all we are and have is from God.

I recall coming home one evening from the office and finding a large box on the dining room table addressed to me. It was from a lady in the church where I grew up whom I hadn't seen in years. I anxiously opened the box to find three suits in it. They had belonged to her son, a businessman in Arizona. All three were in perfect condition. They were exactly the styles I liked and they fit me to a tee. No alterations needed!

During those manna years, God clothed our daughter with beautiful, hardly worn hand-me-downs from a family we had only met once; He answered prayer about tires for our car; He kept old cars nearly maintenance free; and He surprised us with unexpected income just when we needed it. In fact, my wife and I used to joke that if a little extra money came in, it was God's advance warning that the washer was going to break down.

For believers who have a handle on reality, our recognition of God as ultimate provider becomes the joy of a humble spirit. It translates into the freedom of aggressively becoming all that we can possibly become to the praise and honor of His name. It is the esteem of feeling good about ourselves because God is working in us and through us. It is reflected in a strength of character and conviction.

It is not easy, though, to plant that spirit in our being. I recently saw a handsome, muscular guy wearing a T-shirt that said *It's hard for someone like me to be humble.* No doubt that's what T.S. Eliot was getting at when he wrote, "Humility is the most difficult of all virtues to achieve; nothing dies harder than the desire to think well of oneself."

When that young church was ready to apply to the local bank for the financing of our first building project, we approached the bank president with a detailed portfolio of our financial history. The banker looked carefully through it and admiringly remarked, "Somebody carries a big stick at your church." One church member replied, "The Lord has been good to meet all of our needs." The banker responded, "Yes, but He couldn't have done it without you." The reality of the matter is that He *could* have!

Yielding to the reality of God's work as provider and sustainer reflects positively in our speech. It automatically cancels boasting, exaggerating, flattery, and complaining. In their place will come speech that submits to our God-caused lot in life and tactfully gives Him the credit. We will:

- tactfully give God the credit for what we are, have, and have accomplished
- tactfully give God the credit for the good we see in others
- encourage others to recognize God's place as sovereign provider in their lives
- reflect spirits of gratefulness to God in every circumstance

Humility gladly submits to God's rightful place as Lord. It produces a right spirit toward others and a grateful sense of submission to God's providing work on our behalf. A living commitment to humility revolutionizes our speech. It causes us to consistently speak out for the *real* Number One.

9

DEFUSING ANGER

Douse the fire in your tongue

Patience—if it is a virtue, then anger is a vice. Anger is what takes over when patience has run out. The story is told of the teacher who patiently put boots on 32 children. After the last boot went on the 32nd student the child said, "These aren't my boots." The teacher, now out of patience, ripped the boots off. The child continued, "They are my sister's; she let me wear them today."

Impatience is the prelude to an angry spirit which often vents itself in angry words. Angry words are the noxious smoke from the fire in our hearts. Henry Ward Beecher said it well when he quipped, "Speak when you are angry and you'll make the best speech you'll ever regret."

Scripture is full of illustrations of angry responses and angry words. Anger was Cain's response to God's rejection of his sacrifice (Gen. 4:5). King Saul's anger was kindled because his throne was threatened by David. "Whatever Saul sent him to do, David did it so successfully that Saul gave him a high rank in the army. This pleased all the people, and Saul's officers as well. When the men were returning home after David had killed the Philistine, the women came out from all the towns of Israel to meet King Saul with singing and dancing, with joyful songs and with tambourines and lutes. As they danced, they sang: 'Saul has slain his thousands, and David his tens of thousands.' Saul was very angry; this refrain galled him. 'They have credited David with tens of thousands,' he thought, 'but me with only thousands. What more can he get but the kingdom?' And from that time on Saul kept a jealous eye on David" (1 Sam. 18:5-9).

Jonah's anger was kindled against God when God didn't perform the way Jonah wanted Him to (Jonah 4). His anger led to threatening words with a suicidal flair. All because he didn't get his own way.

The disciples became indignant about the fact that the mother of James and John had asked for positions of power and prestige for her sons in the coming kingdom (Matt. 20:20-28). They were indignant because they wanted those positions of status for themselves. It was a thwarted desire for gain and advancement that kindled their anger.

The elder son (Luke 15:11-32) spoke angrily to his father because, as he compared himself with his brother, he felt he had been unfairly treated, when in reality he possessed all of his father's inheritance.

Rejection, jealousy, disappointment, thwarted gain, and ungrateful comparison are all real sources of anger. Unfortunately, anger never lives in isolation. It is like a cancer that gnaws at us. For Cain it meant murdering his brother, which resulted in inner fear, alienation, and God's judgment. Saul's anger caused him to brood and be depressed. It resulted in deep hatred for David.

Jonah's anger turned inward and Godward as he became a victim of self-pity, depression, and thoughts of suicide. The disciples' anger brought division and strife to that important group that desperately needed to be unified. And the elder son's anger alienated him from his father, who was the source of his sustenance and future inheritance.

Anger becomes a social problem with far-reaching effects when it vents itself through words. How can angry words be changed into constructive words of peace and reconciliation? By replacing an angry spirit with a patient spirit. In the New Testament, there are two primary words for *patience*. One carries the thought of not returning harm to those who have harmed us, even though it is within our power to do so. The other reflects the ability to maintain a good spirit even while under pressure.

Both of these dimensions of patience are opposite our natural reactions. We *want* to retaliate when we're crossed, hurt, or reproved. Staying under the pressure graciously till God's work is complete is equally as challenging. When life gets tight, we often pray for relief instead of grace. We are like wet watermelon seeds under the pressure of someone's thumb— we tend to quickly squirt out. And, if we can't escape the pressure, we become angry with the forces that hold us there.

God's Word is highly instructive in regard to successfully applying both dimensions of patience to an angry spirit. Unfortunately, some people have let their anger go unchecked for so long that their anger is deeply ingrained in them. These are what we term "angry people." Counseling with a biblically sensitive Christian therapist may be necessary to deal effectively with such long-standing anger.

But even for "angry" people there are important insights from God's Word that, when applied, bring awareness, sensitivity, and peace.

First, we must realize that anger is a valid, God-given emotion. God gives it to us so we will know right from wrong. Righteous anger is an intense sense of justice.

Anger is what we might call a "signal" emotion. It alerts us to injustice, ungodliness, and unrighteousness. Scripture refers often to God's anger. God is sinless, yet He possesses the capacity for anger. Anger is basically a righteous response to that which is wrong. We become confused when we associate anger with manifestations of unchecked anger that are clearly termed as sin in Scripture. The task of the growing believer is to successfully separate anger from the sins that often accompany it. God intended anger to alert us to unrighteousness—not to lead us into it. Our anger must be listened to and then used to move us to constructive responses. Instead of it maturing into abusive, violent, self-destructive responses, anger can stimulate prayer, concern, corrective action, and a special trust in God that permits us to love our enemies and enjoy inner peace.

Three commands in the New Testament enable us to respond constructively to anger. All three involve the application of patience.

1. *Be slow to anger* (James 1:19). This step develops our ability to handle anger when it first begins to rise. It equips us to evaluate what has happened and what our response should be.

2. *Sin not* (Eph. 4:26). As a part of our evaluation we must be very much aware of the sins that so easily attach themselves to anger. An awareness of them equips us to recognize and resist them.

3. *Deal with anger before sundown* (Eph. 4:26). We can learn how to put anger away by directing our focus toward God and our constructive energy toward the source of the anger. This step applies positive responses that bring inner peace and the potential of healing to an angry encounter.

Hesitate—Evaluate

Be slow to anger is James' command to believers under persecution and trials (James 1:19). It's the biblical equivalent of the old "count to 10" routine. Literally, the word *slow* means to hesitate or delay. This wise advice really asks us to be patient. It urges us to wait under the pressure with a good spirit while seeking a constructive response. Retarding the speed of anger is accomplished by hesitating long enough to carefully evaluate the situation.

There are at least five constructive perspectives which help us to hesitate and evaluate our anger:

1. *God's statements to angry people provide three standards of evaluation.*

    A. "Why are you angry? If you do what is right, will you not be accepted?" were God's questions to Cain (Gen. 4:6-7). If our anger is a response to reproof, to a situation in which we have been wrong, then we must honestly evaluate, humbly repent, and seek to do what is right. Our anger will turn to a patient, humble expression of reconciliation.

    B. "Have you any right to be angry?" was God's question to Jonah (Jonah 4:4). Jonah was angry because God had been merciful. He wanted God to perform according to his own desires. But Jonah had no right to be angry—Nineveh was God's responsibility. Assuming responsibility that doesn't belong to us is often a wrong cause for anger. Patiently submitting to God's will, though sometimes unpleasant for us, develops the patience that will produce words of loyalty and expressions that reflect His grace.

    C. To the angry, elder brother, the father said, "My son, you are always with me, and everything I have is yours" (Luke 15:31). Anger that comes from the self-pity of comparison ignores all the good things for which we can be grateful. It is good for us, on the first sense of anger, to measure whether our anger grows out of a self-centered, unloving comparison with others. Granted, it is difficult to "rejoice with them that do rejoice" (Rom. 12:15, KJV) but a continued focus on all we have to be grateful for will quell the anger of an unloving spirit of discontent.

2. *Do I have sufficient facts to justify my anger?* is a key question in the slowing of our anger. Seeking to understand both sides of a matter is of utmost importance. This kind of patience not only slows anger, but also reflects itself in words that show self-control and the integrity of a fair spirit.

3. *Seeking to understand the situation from the other point of view* is also an effective way to slow anger. Often, mentally placing yourself in the environment of your adversary (the one who has made you angry) defuses the anger and kindles a spirit of patience and tolerance. This kind of patience is called *gentleness* in Galatians 5:23.

4. *Pinpointing the specific cause of anger* will enable you to deal with it immediately. Figure A lists 10 common sources of anger and some basic elements of a constructive response.

5. *Verbalize the sense of oncoming anger.* It's amazing how effective it is to honestly admit that you are feeling angry. But honestly admitting your angry feelings isn't easy. We are normally very defensive about our feelings. I guess it's a matter of pride, but it's hard to say, "I am angry." If I am a little "hot under the collar" about something and my wife asks, "Why are you so angry?" my retort may be a quick heated, "I'm not angry!" That response is not only dishonest, but it's liable to strike a note of anger in my wife's heart as well.

Honestly replying, "I'm not sure, but I do feel angry. Be patient with me until I can get this whole thing in perspective and pray that I can find a constructive response" diffuses the

SOURCE OF ANGER	APPLICATION OF PATIENCE
Stress from an unorganized life or a life that is overcommitted to low priority involvements.	Organize, quit low priority involvements, and practice saying "No" once a day.
Slothful patterns that leave important matters undone or unfinished.	Work hard at priority matters.
Personal guilt.	Seek forgiveness from God and others. Begin to apply principles of victory to that particular weakness.
Righteousness and justice violated.	Commit judgment to God (Rom. 12: 17-21) and turn the energy of your anger into constructive resolution of the problem.
Symbolic anger—transferring anger from past nonrelated incidents that remind you of the present situation.	Recognize the sin of bitterness in your own heart (Heb. 12:15); understand that it is unfair to punish someone because of the past mistakes of others; if necessary, seek the help of a competent counselor.
Residual anger— unresolved situations from previously repeated incidents.	Deal with the recurring problem at a neutral time with open, nondefensive communication. Seek the help of a competent, neutral third party if necessary.
Expectations unfulfilled.	Expect to glorify God (Phil. 1:19).
Rights violated.	Yield your rights to God (Rom. 12:17-21) who will provide for all your needs. If necessary, appeal to the proper authorities (government, parents, boss).
Imposed crises that are out of your control.	Trust the sovereign design of God and submit to His plan. Seek creative ways to glorify God in the suffering (Job 1–2; Phil. 1:20-21, 27-29; 1 Peter 2: 19-25).
Thwarted plans and dreams for self-advancement.	Evaluate the true value of the dreams in relationship to eternal values; submit to God's wise plan for your life.

Figure A.

strength of the anger and begins to turn your heart to positive resolutions.

As the anger comes, these five steps of patience will slow the process down and provide time for us to integrate the whole picture and discern a constructive, godly response. The writer of Proverbs says, "Better a patient man than a warrior, a man who controls his temper than one who takes a city" (Prov. 16:32).

Be Angry and Sin Not

The second command in relationship to anger is, "in your anger do not sin" (Eph. 4:26). Understanding that anger is a signal emotion is of great help. Anger alerts us that something has gone wrong—that justice and righteousness have been violated. However, if anger is not responded to with a patient, "slow down" spirit, it will quickly lead us into sin.

This verse draws a clear distinction between anger and sin. Anger in and of itself is not sin. Sin is what happens when anger is not handled properly. It's like temptation and sin. It is not a sin to be tempted; sin is what happens when temptation goes unchecked (James 1:14-15). Anger is like mayonnaise—a sandwich without it loses its edge. But if it isn't eaten immediately, it will spoil and produce gastronomic misery.

If we *remain* angry and do not do what is right, sin is like a crouching beast waiting to devour us (Gen. 4:7). As Paul says, Satan gets an advantage in our lives (Eph. 4:26-27). Anger that remains becomes spoiled and turns into the self-destructive sins of bitterness and hatred. In fact, many sins are born from residual anger. Speech sins like lying, slander, murmuring, threatening, cursing, taking God's name in vain, and contentious words are all products of anger gone sour. Murder, envy, immorality, division, strife, and revenge are common sins of an angry heart. The writer of the Book of

Hebrews encourages us to "make every effort to live in peace with all men and to be holy; without holiness no one will see the Lord. See to it that no one misses the grace of God and that no bitter root grows up to cause trouble and defile many" (Heb. 12:14-15).

Patiently slowing down the anger to hesitate and evaluate will guard us from anger sins. Instead of angry words that cause turmoil, inner guilt, and social alienation, our lips will project constructive, patient, healing words. Our words will reflect:

- an honest admission of our angry feelings
- requests for prayer support to resist the sins that accompany anger
- requests for godly counsel to respond to anger properly
- nonjudgmental questions that bring sufficient facts to light
- humble repentance when the anger situation is a result of our wrongdoing or self-centeredness
- encouragement to others to hesitate, evaluate, and reject "anger" sins
- the gentleness of an understanding heart that sees the situation from the other point of view
- glory to God by submitting to His perfect plan
- silence. Until we can speak constructive words, silence is truly golden (Ps. 141:3)

In the summertime it's my job to barbecue the steaks. My problem is controlling the heat of the flames. If I can't keep the fire under control, it ruins the meat. Some time ago we bought a grill with a lid on it. Closing the lid while the steaks are cooking reduces the oxygen flow to the flames and enables the embers to be transformed from a destructive force to a constructive, controlled heat that transforms the steaks into a delightful dinner.

The patience to hesitate, evaluate, and reject anger sins puts the lid on the flames. It gives us the opportunity to transform the destructive force of our anger into words that are tastefully seasoned, enjoyable to hear, and a positive contribution to the health of those around us.

10

PATIENCE APPLIED

Good words for bad deeds

Early one Sunday morning as I arrived at the church, I went to the business office to look through Saturday's mail. Without thinking, I turned the key in the door and to my surprise set off the burglar alarm. I almost had a coronary right on the spot. Clanging bells began to blare both inside and out. I panicked—the entire neighborhood would now be awakened at 7 A.M. Sunday morning; the police would probably be called; and I had no idea how to shut it off!

Anger is like that. Unsuspectingly, a key is turned in our lives and the blaring alarm goes off both inside and out. We panic and tighten up. The tranquility of the people around us is shattered. Unfortunately, we have no idea how to shut it off.

To my relief, the custodian came running; took a special key from his key ring and turned the alarm system off.

The alarm is not meant to clang on forever and ever. Once it does its job, it needs to be turned off. If it is not, it becomes a major source of frustration and conflict for all who are within earshot. Anger is like an alarm. It is a signal emotion.

It alerts us, that we might respond constructively. After we have hesitated and evaluated, avoiding anger sins, we must put the anger away and respond constructively.

That is why God commands, "Do not let the sun go down while you are still angry" (Eph. 4:26). I am thankful that God understands how difficult it can be for us to extinguish our anger. It often takes time and hard spiritual work. Repeated applications of biblical principles are normally required to put our anger to rest. God graciously gives us till the end of the day.

Other passages emphasize the importance of turning anger off quickly. Psalm 37:8 says to "cease from anger, and forsake wrath" (KJV) while Ephesians 4:31 warns, "Get rid of all bitterness, rage and anger, brawling and slander, along with every form of malice."

I had only been in the pastorate a short time when Barbara, a young married woman, came to see me. She related how she had grown to dislike her husband. As she put it, "I just don't love him anymore." She could no longer stand to be near him. She cringed when he touched her. Barbara looked at me and asked, "What can I do?" As we talked, it became clear that she struggled with a lot of unresolved pent-up anger. I asked her to come back next week with a list of the ways in which her husband irritated her. I was buying time. I really didn't know what to say. She needed the key to put anger away. I was being asked to find it for her.

The next week Barbara related that she was more angry now than ever. She had a list of 33 irritations. The more she had written, the worse she felt. She read me a few of her frustrations: he would come home from work, grab the newspaper without saying anything, read it until supper, ungratefully inhale the food, and finish the night in front of the TV; he was always late; he often criticized her in public, and on went the list.

During the week between appointments, it became plain to me that God had indeed provided some practical keys to keep the sun from going down on our wrath. As she began to work through these keys, her heart grew warm toward Jim. Today they live in a restored happy relationship.

Jim came to me one day and said, "I really like what you guys are doing with my wife!" I said, "You guys?" to which he replied, "Yeah, you and God!" The day she said to me, "Pastor, I think I have the most wonderful husband in the world" was the day I knew that God's keys to turning anger off really work.

There are many keys that people use to deal with their anger. Since some of us think that a good Christian doesn't have anger, we repress it, trying to pretend it doesn't exist. This is not only unscriptural and dishonest but it is also physiologically and psychologically dangerous. As someone well said, "When I repress my emotions, my stomach keeps score." You will become like a time bomb looking for a place to explode.

Hence, many therapists tell us not to repress our anger, but to ventilate it. To let it *all* out. If you feel like yelling and screaming, do it! You'll feel better. Well, it may help *you* to feel momentarily better, but you'll soon regret the words and actions of your rage. Seeds of resentment and distrust will be planted in the hearts of those who were victimized by your ventilation. In her article in the November 1982 issue of *Psychology Today,* social psychologist Carol Tavris states, "People who are most prone to give vent to their rage get angrier, not less angry" ("Anger Defused," Carol Tavris, *Psychology Today,* Nov., 1982, pp. 25-31).

Though some suggest that ventilating alone (beating your pillow, screaming in a locked room) may be a helpful release, it doesn't deal with the issue that creates the anger.

God's Word commands us to deal decisively with our anger.

We should not bottle it up or carelessly ventilate it at will; we must respond from God's point of view. A composite understanding of Scripture demonstrates that turning our anger off demands redirecting our focus and our energy. This is the key that turned Barbara's destructive anger into productive patience.

Redirecting Our Focus

When we become angry, our natural tendency is to mentally and emotionally focus on the *source* of our anger. In fact, angry people become locked into bondage with the source of their anger. The person or situation that has stimulated the anger becomes an overriding preoccupation. We take those with whom we are angry everywhere we go. We plan what we will say, what they will say, and what we will say in reply. We fantasize all kinds of schemes of revenge. We actually become servants to the focus of our anger.

This focus of anger will move through a five step process. At first, we will *fret* about the problem. To fret is to anxiously mull it over in our minds. The fretting will then mature to *envy*. Perhaps we will be envious of how nicely our wives treat others or of how much time our husbands spend at the office. Cain was envious of Abel; Joseph's brothers of his relationship to his father; Jonah of God's mercy toward Nineveh; and the elder brother of the way his younger brother was treated. The envy quickly turns to *anger,* which is the "slow burn." Anger permitted to remain, sours into *wrath* (the explosion), and wrath matures into a plotting to carry out revenge, which is the step of *evil.*

The evil we do in return is not done because we are so nasty, but rather to protect us from further offense, to carry out justice, and to force change in the behavior patterns of those who hurt us. Many times that evil response is expressed through our words—words that use expletives to diminish the other individual's worth; words that threaten; words that cut; and words that heap guilt on the one causing our pain.

The "fret-envy-anger-wrath-evil" cycle of our focus runs its course like this: Being concerned about your marriage's lack of romance, it's like an answer to prayer that your husband asks you out to dinner for two on Friday night. You decide that you would rather enjoy candlelight for two at home with your favorite recipes. It would make a good prelude to a special evening. Friday morning, as he goes out the door, you remind him "dinner for two at 7:00." "I can't wait" is his reply. As the children come home from school, you feed them early and send them to bed. The table is set; the food smells fantastic; there's a fire in the fireplace, soft music, the candles are lit and it's 7 o'clock.

7:10—FRET—You wonder what has happened—a traffic jam—an accident?

7:30—ENVY—If it had been an accident, the police would have notified you by now. You think, *That's how much I'm worth. His business gets more time than I do. I'll bet he wasn't late to his lunch appointment. He's more considerate of his secretary than he is of me.*

7:45—ANGER—You begin to feel tense and hostile. You are well into the slow burn.

8:00—WRATH—As you hear the car coming in the driveway, you quickly scrape the food off your plate and put your plate back on the table. Taking his plate of food, you hold it under the turned up air conditioner to cool it down "real good" and then set it down at his place.

8:03—EVIL—As he walks in the door, he gets what he deserves. The treatment may be varied—

silence, an angry outburst of words and
tears, limited cold conversation, or whatever works best.

Unfortunately, though he has been insensitive and irre-
sponsible (he could have at least called), the husband becomes
defensive and instead of humbly repenting, he clams up; turns
around and leaves; or stands his ground and fights. The much
hoped for revival of romance has made romance all the more
distant.

There must be a better way. There is. Psalm 37 drops us
right into an anger situation. The psalmist speaks to those
who are the victims of "evil men" and "those who do wrong"
(Ps. 37:1). In the course of the first 11 verses, the text teaches
us the proper response. Initially, the psalmist tells us that
fretting (v. 1), envy (v. 1), anger (v. 8), wrath (v. 8), and
evil (v. 8) are out-of-bounds from God's point of view.

Constructively, the text gives five positive responses that
replace the damaging "fret-envy-anger-wrath-evil" syndrome.
These five steps liberate our focus from the source of our
anger and redirect it to God who is the solution to our anger.
They are trust (v. 3), delight (v. 4), commit (v. 5), be still
(v. 7), and wait patiently (v. 7).

Trust. Trusting God means to lean on four firm realities
that are rooted in God's character and His Word. First, that
God is just. Justice is of absolute importance to Him. When
wrong is done, He is acutely aware of it. Second, His Word
promises that He will repay the wrongs that have been done.
Third, He promises to effectively work to change the lives of
those who do wrong. Fourth, God seeks to protect those who
trust in Him. Passages such as Genesis 18:25, Romans 12:17-
21, Hebrews 12:5-11, Proverbs 3:11-12, 18:10 all fortify our
ability to trust God in these areas. As we trust God in these
four dimensions we no longer need to feel that we must

retaliate to even the score (justice), effect change, or protect ourselves. They are God's responsibilities. Recognizing them as God's responsibilities and believing that God will care for them is step one of a successful focus toward God.

Delight. This delight is kindled in two areas. We are reminded in Scripture that God brings trials into our lives to refine and mature us (James 1). Pressure builds character. Though often not an emotional delight, mentally we can reckon the pressure to be a positive instrument in the hand of God on our behalf. The second aspect of this delight is the assurance that God will work in the life of my offender in His wise time.

Commit. After successfully trusting and delighting, you can expect Satan to whisper in your ear, "Are you going to let them get away with that?" or "You are becoming too vulnerable—fight back!" I find that I must recommit myself time and time again to a Godward focus in regard to the same event. If you were keeping a chart of the time of your commitment, for a 7:45 offense you may need to commit yourself to focus on God at 8:05, 8:07, and 9:23.

Be still. At this point, a sense of stillness and peace should set up residence in your spirit. As long as you are trusting, delighting in, and committing yourself to the Lord, inner peace will be your reward. You have now effectively turned the anger off by transferring the situation to God through a redirection of your focus.

Wait patiently. It may be difficult to keep your focus locked on God. The gravity of the flesh will seek to pull it down into the bondage of the offender again. One strength that this gravity has is the strength of time. If God does not seem to change the situation as quickly as we would like, we revert back to the old "fret-envy-anger-wrath-evil" cycle. Waiting patiently means a commitment to these five steps regardless of God's timing. We must yield to God's work in His way and in His time.

We must recognize that some of God's work may not be done until the final judgment. In the meantime the maintenance of our focus toward Him enables us to enjoy peace, a clear conscience, and a deepening maturity in our experience. Our commitment ultimately rests not on God's action but, rather on our desire to obey Him.

Sally, whose husband was carrying on an affair with their babysitter, committed herself to these principles. Though it was difficult, she experienced peace, a clear conscience, and the maturity that the process brings. As a part of her commitment, she memorized Psalm 37:1-11. One night, she succumbed to the gravity of the flesh and shifted her focus back to her husband. As you can imagine, it ignited a great explosion which was vented through angry words. She told me later that, as she was enjoying the luxury of the verbal ventilation, suddenly the words of Psalm 37 (Trust-Delight-Commit-Rest-Wait Patiently) flashed across her mind like a neon sign. "It took all the fun out of it," she confessed. She regrouped and enjoyed afresh the peace of trusting in God.

This Godward response triggers the patience that withholds retaliation when it is within our power to retaliate.

Redirecting Our Energy

The second dimension of redirected anger is a step of spiritual assertiveness. It involves taking the energy that comes with anger and using it for constructive resolution. Successfully dealing with anger demands not only transferring the situation to God, but constructive action toward the source of our anger.

Psalm 37:3 and Romans 12:17-21 both indicate the necessity of a positive response to those who are the source of our anger. Doing good (Ps. 37:3) encompasses at least four crucial responses.

Positive actions. Forgiveness is now possible since I know that God will deal with my offender and use the offense in a positive way in my life. When I am reminded of the source of my anger, it becomes an opportunity to commit myself afresh to a Godward focus and seek measures to heal the offender (Eph. 4:31-32; 1 Peter 2:19-25).

In addition to a forgiving spirit, reaching back in love is demanded. "Do not repay anyone evil for evil. Be careful to do what is right in the eyes of everybody. If it is possible, as far as it depends on you, live at peace with everyone. Do not take revenge, my friends, but leave room for God's wrath, for it is written: 'It is mine to avenge; I will repay,' says the Lord. On the contrary: 'If your enemy is hungry, feed him; if he is thirsty, give him something to drink. In doing this, you will heap burning coals on his head.' Do not be overcome by evil, but overcome evil with good" (Rom. 12:17-21). Paul is speaking here about the love that meets genuine need. Being sensitive to the needs of our enemies is the essence of Christ's exhortation to "love your enemies" (Matt. 5:44). Meeting an enemy's needs and praying for him are strong forms of therapy.

Barbara sought to restore her love for her husband by developing a disciplined Godward focus; she sought ways to express God's love to him. She began praying for Jim and took positive steps to meet his needs (genuine love). As she took away the verbal pressure, God worked some special changes in his life. She rushed to me one Sunday morning and said, "Pastor, you'll never guess what happened this week. Jim left the newspaper outside, walked right into the kitchen, and asked me how my day had been!" God had been busy in his heart. Positive actions are the right reactions to an angry situation.

Honest reactions. In addition to positive actions, we must redirect our energy by honestly communicating about our hurts with the one who has hurt us. This is not always easy, but if our spirits are solidly locked into the "trust-delight-commit-rest-wait patiently" routine, then we can say what we feel without appearing judgmental (which would put the other individual on the defensive). When we communicate with our offenders, we should keep several points in mind.

Choice of time and place can make or break the encounter. It is usually unwise to confront the offender when he is actually doing something that offends you. At a neutral time, you might say, "I have something that is important to me that I need to talk to you about. Let's have coffee together." This will catch their curiosity.

Determine to be totally open and non-defensive and choose words that communicate those attitudes. Questions that give people a chance to explain their point of view are helpful. Something like, "What did you have in mind when you said that to me?" is a question that opens the door to understanding.

Humility to admit your part in the problem will often enable them to admit their shortcomings as well.

Stating the way you view the situation without projecting blame will help them to understand you.

Commit yourself not to permit the conversation to deteriorate into a revival of anger.

Maintain your commitment to the "trust-delight-commit-rest-wait patiently" perspective so that if the conversation is not successful your trust is still in the Lord to intercede. This is crucial to blocking the reentry of anger into your spirit.

Responsible Reaction. Discerning our responsibility to actively right the wrong is an important step in redirecting our energy. God has ordained certain authorities to exercise discipline toward those who have been unjust and unrighteous. Government, the church, parents, and employers are all recognized channels of authority. An appeal to any of these is legitimate when the offense is something that involves them. However, we must remember that God has many unseen options to do His work of justice and discipline. Any step toward personal involvement should be done with prayer, discernment, and patience.

Exhaustion Reaction. Physical activity can also be a very constructive way to redirect anger. I have a friend who jogs and meditates on the constructive responses that he can have toward problems. Some housewives clean their entire houses with the residual energy of their anger. Housecleaning gives good opportunity to pray and plan for constructive responses as well.

Redirecting our focus and our energy gives birth to patience in our hearts. Patience rejects angry words and replaces them with words that:
- reflect a forgiving spirit (Eph. 4:31-32)
- are constructive
- lead to resolution
- are nonjudgmental
- reflect a confidence in God's ultimate resolution of the problem
- are sensitively timed
- are sensitive to the needs of others, even the needs of our offenders
- allow a peaceful silence for God to do His work
- testify to the positive hope of God's work in our lives as well as the lives of our offenders

Patience is the virtue that transforms an angry tongue. Patience takes time to hesitate and evaluate. It rejects anger sins. True patience finds its strength is an unflinching focus on God and an unconditional love toward those who have hurt us.

11

THE TRUST-LOVE LIFE

Conquer fear with love

Fear is a crippler. I can remember, as a little boy, the times I found it hard to sleep because of my fear of the dark. That fear played all kinds of tricks on me: my clothes thrown on the chair looked like a monster in the shadows; under my bed I imagined snakes and alligators; and who knew what lived way down at the foot of the bed between my sheets? Because of fear, I couldn't sleep. I had no relief until my father would hear my call and turn on the lights. The light dispelled the darkness and cancelled the fear.

We never outgrow our vulnerability to fear. Fear paralyzes our spirits so that we are unable to do some of the most important things that contribute to spiritual maturity and vitality, not the least of which is the ability to speak words of courage and love. Because of fear, some of us are afraid to tell others about Christ, afraid to exercise our spiritual gifts, afraid to extend our lives and resources to the benefit of others, and afraid to venture into new areas of growth and discovery. Fear paralyzes us spiritually and leaves us vulnerable to Satan's attacks. If a young woman fears the loss of a boyfriend, that fear may lead her to do things that she knows are opposed to God's will. Fear of separation and the unknown has kept many from serving the Lord overseas. Fear of the loss of prestige, money, power, status, and friends has caused some to compromise biblical convictions and a righteous standing before God.

Granted, some types of fear are healthy and used by God for our benefit. The fear of falling makes us cautious on ladders; the fear of pain keeps our hands off the hot stove; and the fear of failure often keeps us diligent in our work. But there is a vast arena in which Satan uses fear to pull the strings of our lives.

It is no wonder that fear has a string tied to our tongues as well. As we have discovered, many communication sins find their stimulus in a spirit of fear.

What is the biblical cure for a fearful spirit? What will enable us to transform our fearful words to words of love and courage? There are two steps that we can take to topple fear from the throne of our existence. They are the steps of developing the skills of trust and love.

Emotionally, fear focuses on protecting and preserving me. It is self-centered. While at times this kind of fear can be constructive (fear of fire, fear of wild beasts), it often surfaces in destructive ways. It shows itself in the self-centeredness of not using our words to witness because we are afraid of losing friends and social standing. Fearing the loss of a promotion, we may self-centeredly compromise our ethics both verbally and morally to gain business success. When others get in the way of our plans and desires, we may verbally intimidate or abuse them to get them out of our paths. We fear that our desires may be unfulfilled.

What corrals and transforms this self-centered fear? The genuine love that commits itself to God's will and others' needs (1 John 4:18, NASB).

Often, however, trust must precede love. Trusting in God to care for me frees me from self-interest so that I am able to care for others. If I assume that I am solely responsible to protect and preserve all that I am, have, or will become, then fear will dominate me. When outside forces threaten some aspect of my present existence or future dreams, then I must stand alone against them. If these forces are greater than I, then fear becomes a moving force that manipulates my responses. Trusting in God to protect and provide dispels this fear (Ps. 56:3).

To freely witness to my lost friend requires faith in God's power to convince and convict. To share financially in the needs of another requires trust in God's promise to meet my needs. To remove fear from difficult obedience requires trust in God's wisdom, protection, and power.

Activating a biblical blend of trust and love is the key to power over fear. It is the key to words of courage and grace. How do we develop the skills of trust and love?

The Trust Factor

Why did the Israelites murmur and complain in the wilderness when the 10 spies brought their report from the Promised Land? Why did Rahab lie to the soldiers? Why did Peter curse, swear, and deny the Lord in the courtyard of the chief priest?

Israel, Rahab, and Peter were locked into the fear of godless self-concern and it showed in their words. Each of them could have trusted in God and given courageous testimony to their faith in a God who delights in delivering His own. Each of them knew that God had accomplished deliverance before. But they lapsed into the assumption that they had to protect themselves as though God would not.

By contrast, Shadrach, Meshach, and Abednego in the face of the fiery furnace rejected the fear of self-concern and trusted totally in God. They said, "O Nebuchadnezzar, we do not need to defend ourselves before you in this matter. If we are thrown into the blazing furnace, the God we serve is able to save us from it, and He will rescue us from your hand, O King. But even if He does not, we want you to know, O King, that we will not serve your gods or worship the image of gold you have set up" (Dan. 3:16-18). Their trust was unlimited and unconditional. They would trust in their God even if He didn't deliver them. Their fearless words reflect complete trust in the power of God and His worthiness to be worshipped and served regardless of the outcome.

The psalmist declared, "When I am afraid, I will trust in You. In God, whose word I praise, in God I trust; I will not be afraid. What can mortal man do to me? Then my enemies will turn back when I call for help. By this I will know that God is for me. In God, whose word I praise, in the Lord, whose word I praise—in God I trust; I will not be afraid. What can man do to me?" (Ps. 56:3-4, 9-11)

God's character provides four handles for our trust to hold in the face of fear. They are the reality of God's presence, power, protection, and provision.

The Presence of God. As a boy I can remember visiting a church on a Sunday evening in one of the worst sections of New York City. Our family parked a block or so away. As we walked, fear grew steadily in my heart. Thankfully we made it safely to the church and enjoyed the service. After the service, the pastor asked two of his deacons to escort us back to the car. They looked like the church "bouncers." Though it was dark outside, I had no fear. What made the difference? The presence of those who could protect me.

Scripture is full of calls to trust in the presence of God in times of fear. Joshua was commanded not to be terrified "for the Lord your God will be with you wherever you go" (Josh: 1:9). In the shepherd's psalm we are told to fear no evil because God is with us (Ps. 23:4). The Book of Hebrews encourages boldness in our spirits by declaring, "God has said, 'Never will I leave you; never will I forsake you.' So we say with confidence, 'The Lord is my helper; I will not be afraid. What can man do to me?' " (Heb. 13:5-6)

The Power of God. God is not just a God of unlimited power. He is a God who delights in sharing His power on behalf of His people. His power dwells within us to enable us to witness (Acts 1:8). It dwells in His Word to convict and transform us (Heb. 4:12). The power of God is spent to supply our needs (Phil. 4:19); to give us strength in trouble (2 Cor. 12:8-10); to keep us from temptations and trials that would be beyond our ability to cope (1 Cor. 10:13); and to provide escape mechanisms in those temptations that He permits (10:13). The shared strength of God disarms any intimidating influence in our environment. "God has not given us the spirit of fear; but of power, and of love, and of a sound mind (2 Tim. 1:7, KJV).

The Protection of God. Throughout Scripture God is clearly portrayed as a protector. Israel was protected many times against military odds far beyond their ability. Jesus Christ walked through hostile mobs untouched. Though God chose to take some servants home and to permit others to go through suffering (Heb. 11:35-38), He does activate His protecting power when that is in the best interest of His plan. Many of God's protective interventions have been dramatic. His protection of Sarah was especially so (Gen. 20). When she entered King Abimelech's harem, God protected Sarah by closing all the wombs of the king's house and striking the king deathly ill. God takes special delight in protecting those who trust Him. If He chooses not to protect us from troubling circumstances, He then protects us with His grace to cope (2 Cor. 12:7-10).

Psalm 91 pictures God as a protecting refuge. "He who

dwells in the shelter of the Most High will rest in the shadow of the Almighty. I will say of the Lord, 'He is my refuge and my fortress, my God, in whom I trust' " (vv. 1-2).

The Provision of God. God provides grace to enable us to go through circumstances that would normally defeat us with fear. God provides His Word, which assures us of the fullness of His character and gives us the principles to follow in the face of fear. He provides the supportive fellowship of fellow believers who pray for and with us. The indwelling Spirit, who prays for us, guides us, and teaches us, provides the assurance that He will meet all of our needs.

The kind of trust that dismisses fear is a committed trust— not in ourselves—but in God's presence, shared power, protection, and provision. This trust will be reflected in words of courage, loyalty, and commitment regardless of the odds that we face. A trusting heart will eliminate doubting, murmuring, angry, lying, jealous, slandering, and gossiping words and replace them with words that:

- affirm commitment to righteousness at all cost
- give testimony to God's sufficiency
- express loyalty to God and confidence regardless of the circumstance
- express truth in the face of danger
- encourage others to practice the presence, power, protection, and provision of God
- forgive those who hurt and misuse us
- are grateful toward God and those who provide support as we face difficult times
- give testimony of our experiences of deliverance and grace

The Love Factor

Love and fear are mutually exclusive, for complete love drives fear away (1 John 4:18). Fear focuses on my needs; true love focuses on the needs of others. Love is unquestionably more powerful than fear.

God's Word speaks of a kind of love that is different from our cultural impressions of love; it is divine love. It is a love that is sensitive to real needs and is willing to extend our resources to meet those needs (John 3:16; Rom. 5:8). John 15:9-13 clearly teaches that Christ has loved us with divine love and that we are to love one another with that same kind of love. This divine love is even able to conquer the fear of death. This divine love has a dual focus. It is not a response to someone or something. God is love. Because He is love, He extends that love to us. His love has nothing to do with who we are or how we act. He loves us from within Himself. This is why the Cross is possible. Jesus Christ died for us, not because we are worthy, but because He is love. Our love for one another, then, is to be a sharing of God's divine love. Jesus said, "Love each other as I have loved you" (John 15:12). We show concern and care for others because we possess God's kind of love and we extend it to all—unconditionally, regardless of their worth and value. C.S. Lewis, in *Mere Christianity,* says that the "worldly man treats certain people kindly because he likes them; the Christian, trying to treat everyone kindly, finds himself liking more and more people as he goes—including people he could not even have imagined himself liking at the beginning" (*The Best of C.S. Lewis,* The Iversen Associates, p. 505).

Divine love is not an emotional response, but an act of the will. Divine love is expressed not necessarily because we "feel" like it, but because we choose to love. If we wait to "feel" like loving someone, our love will be erratic and arbitrary. Since "God has poured out His love into our hearts" (Rom. 5:5), we possess the ability to give to the needs of others regardless of how we feel.

Divine love stimulates right feelings. The more we love

someone, the better we will feel about them and about ourselves. God's Word says that where our treasures are there our hearts will be also. When we love with the treasures of our time, prayers, and resources, our hearts will follow and soon warm the relationship.

Divine love is focused toward God and toward one another. We love God by giving ourselves willingly to His concerns. "This is love for God: to obey His commands. And His commands are not burdensome" (1 John 5:3). Secondly, divine love is to be shared with one another as the badge of our discipleship. Christ commands us to "love one another. As I have loved you, so must you love one another. All men will know that you are My disciples if you love one another" (John 13:34-35). These two directions of our love are brought together in Christ's statement that we are to love God with all our beings and our neighbors as ourselves (Matt. 22:34-38).

What does all of this have to do with conquering fear? Fear turns our attention inward. It thrives on our self-centeredness—on our concern for our own welfare. On the other hand, divine love turns our attention upward and outward toward the concerns of God and the needs of others.

No wonder John says, "Perfect love drives out fear" (1 John 4:18). When I am trusting in God in every circumstance, I am free then to commit myself in love to the concerns of God and the needs of others without thinking of myself. A conscious commitment to true love will dispel the shackles of self-centered fear.

This commitment to active divine love is beautifully exercised in our speech. One of our greatest capacities to meet needs is through our words—words that are truly the expressions of a loving, caring heart. Unfortunately, we tend to speak empty words and phrases that reflect polite concern while keeping a person's needs at arm's length. We ask, "How are you?" hoping they won't *really* tell us. We must remember the warning of 1 Corinthians 13:1, "If I speak in the tongues of men and of angels, but have not love, I am only a resounding gong or a clanging cymbal." True words of love are willing to help.

What might we look for to determine whether we have true love in our spirits? First Corinthians 13:4-7 lists 14 characteristics of true love. Figure B shows how each characteristic effectively replaces the spirit of fear.

As our hearts beat with love for God and others, the results will soon show in our mouths. These 14 qualities will become evident in pleasant, gracious words that are dynamically used by God to heal, warm, encourage, and excite others to righteousness and faith. A heart of love is evident in our speech in many ways:

Patient. Patience refuses to carry out revenge even when we are able to do so. Patient words of forgiveness, understanding, and love will seek to restore and revitalize relationships that are divided. Patient words genuinely speak to the welfare and prosperity of our adversaries (Matt. 5:43-48; Rom. 12:17-21).

Kind. Kind words reflect a sensitivity to the problems, position, and responsibilities of others. Kindness unfolds in questions that seek to genuinely understand and in words that are soft, gentle, and encouraging.

Not Envious. True love is thrilled to see others prosper and gladly says so. "Congratulations," "Good job," "We are happy for you," "You deserve it," and "We are glad that God chose to bless you like this" are all words of true love.

Not Boastful. A loving spirit gives God the credit for accomplishments and gains.

Humble. A truly humble spirit admits when it is wrong, gives God the credit for personal gain, and speaks words of glad submission to Christ.

Not Self-Seeking. A loving heart silently listens so that it can hear all that another has to say. It is genuinely concerned about those things that are of interest and importance to others.

Not Easily Angered. A heart that is slow to anger hears the whole story and asks questions that bring pertinent facts to the surface so that a wise evaluation and response can be made.

Keeps No Record of Wrong. This love refuses to speak of past negative circumstances. It never says, "I told you so." It has erased the tape of the past and speaks words of encouragement about the future.

Takes No Delight in Evil. This spirit of love eliminates gossip and slander or anything that communicates an evil report about another. It never encourages another person to do wrong and is never glad about another's failure. It communicates grief and sorrow over that which is contrary to God's righteousness. This love produces words that genuinely confront and call to righteousness.

Rejoices in the Truth. Speaking the truth in humility and love is the expression of a loving tongue.

Protects. The protecting tongue responds to negative information by always giving others the benefit of the doubt. The protecting tongue uses statements like "Are you sure you have all the facts?" or "I know that person and I'd be surprised if that were really true." If it *is* true, a loving spirit shows in our tongues by statements like "Let's tell no one else and pray for ways to constructively deal with this matter" or "Why don't we go to this person and hear his side of the story?"

Trusts. Verbalizing that we trust one another is the result of a loving spirit. A trusting tongue rejects words of suspicion, judgment, and doubt, though it is not naive or foolishly vulnerable. It promotes the integrity and virtue of another until proven otherwise.

Heart Level Love		
FEAR Self-Centered	**LOVE'S TRANS-FORMING QUALITY**	**LOVE** Others-Centered
Lashing out to protect myself—fear of vulnerability.	PATIENT	Trusting God to work in my offender's life while doing good to my offender.
Thinking only of myself—being kind to "me" and expecting others to do the same.	KIND	Looking at life from others' point of view and seeking to help them with an understanding spirit.
Fearing personal loss, comparing, wondering why I don't have their good fortune.	NOT ENVIOUS	Rejoicing in the prosperity of others, sharing in their joy.
Drawing attention to myself, fearing loss of acclaim.	NOT BOASTFUL	Focusing on God's goodness to me and the accomplishment of others.
Fearing loss of status and prestige, I do everything I can to put myself ahead.	HUMBLE	Wanting God to be truly first in my life and the lives of others.
Looking out for my best interests and advantage, strong focus on rights and privileges.	NOT SELF-SEEKING	Looking out for the best interests of God and others.
Quick to defend my personal territory, dreams, and desires.	NOT EASILY ANGERED	Hesitates and evaluates each situation from God's point of view and the point of view of others.

Figure B

Heart Level Love		
FEAR **Self-Centered**	**LOVE'S TRANS-FORMING QUALITY**	**LOVE** **Others-Centered**
Remembers past offenses to use as ammunition in the future to defend, intimidate, or control.	KEEPS NO RECORD OF WRONG	Forgives for the sake of another and doesn't seek to control through past offenses.
Uses evil schemes and words to protect and enhance personal position and personal gain.	TAKES NO DELIGHT IN EVIL	Recognizes that evil is always harmful to everyone involved, willing to refrain for the sake of God and others.
Recognizes the value of truth only when it is convenient, often lies to protect self or gain advantage.	REJOICES IN THE TRUTH	Recognizes the value of truth even if it means admitting to wrongdoing.
In order to protect self, is willing to endanger others both spiritually and physically.	PROTECTS	Desires to shelter others from danger, even at cost to self.
Is suspicious, doubtful, and skeptical, especially in situations that threaten me with some personal loss.	TRUSTS	Willingly trusts in others until proven untrustworthy, seeks to engender trust.
Discourages and belittles others' potential out of the fear of their gain at the expense of position or personal status.	HOPES	Believes in the potential of others and encourages them to discover their potential even if it threatens me.
Stops loving as soon as it becomes too difficult, inconvenient, or undeserved. Fear of becoming used or taken advantage of will quench this kind of love.	PERSEVERES	Loves regardless of external circum-stances or of the worthiness of the object loved. It endures.

Figure B
Continued

Hopes. This love projects vision and hope for the future. It speaks of positive worth and value, the solution of crises, and the possible resolution of problems. It realizes that we can do all things through Christ's strength (Phil. 4:13).

Perseveres. Divine love endures regardless of the circumstances. This shows in words of love toward enemies; continued words of concern for others in times of extended personal crises; and words that express our unconditional commitment to love when under pressure.

A commitment to trust and love dispels the failure of fearful speech and transforms our words into words of grace, concern, and encouragement. There is no better example of a blended "trust-love" life demonstrated in words than the example of Jesus Christ. In a time of great crisis, He trusted in God (1 Peter 2:21-25) and focused on the needs of others. From the cross He said, "Father, forgive them, for they know not what they do" (Luke 23:34, KJV). To John, He instructed that he should care for His mother (John 19: 26-27). For all the world to hear, Jesus said, "It is finished" (v. 30), speaking of His work of love in dying for us. May this mind be in us which was also in Christ Jesus (Phil. 2:5).

Enjoy the fearless beauty of the trust-love blend in your heart and share the joy with others through your words.

12

APPLES OF GOLD

A commitment to positive speech

The joy of a tongue that blesses others from a heart of humility, patience, and love is one of the rewards of the maturing believer. Good words produce inner joy, give strength to others, and invoke the pleasure of the Father. God's Word is full of compliments about the worth of a tongue in check. In Proverbs the productive tongue is characterized as being wise, like choice silver, a banquet for many, the Lord's delight, a guardian of the soul, a vehicle to turn away wrath, a healer, a tree of life, full of knowledge, and a reflection of faithfulness (Prov. 10:19-21; 12:22; 13:3, 15:1, 4; 17:27; 31:26). In fact, God's Word says, "A word fitly spoken is like apples of gold in pictures of silver" (25:11, KJV).

However, as you develop positive speech patterns, you will find that it is challenging to maintain your commitment in a world that has become insensitive to God's perspectives in regard to our talk. A solid commitment in three important areas will guard the sacredness of your words and help you lead others to an experience of healed communication patterns.

Inner Maturity

Your foremost commitment should be to nurture and protect the inward development of humility, patience, and love. These are skills that grow and develop. They are taught by the Spirit through His Word and engrafted into your life by attentive application and continued commitment.

In order to aid in the development of these skills, you should:

Define accurately and practically, in your own words, the essence of humility, patience, and love. Make these definitions concise, biblical, interesting, and relevant. Be creative.

Memorize your definitions and key Scripture passages that fortify your sensitivity to the essence and importance of genuine humility, patience, and the trust-love life.

Pray regularly (several times a day) for the developing work of the Spirit in each of the three areas. Prayer will not only unlock the Spirit's work, but will also help remind you of your commitment.

Speak less and listen more, permitting the principles of humility, patience, and love to guard the door of your lips. David prayed, "Set a guard over my mouth, O Lord; keep watch over the door of my lips" (Ps. 141:3).

Evaluate what you have said by the standards of the three principles that you are now committed to, not by the standards of others.

Be patient. Your spirit and your speech cannot be transformed in a day. Patiently persist!

One great challenge in maintaining your commitment is the challenge of successfully responding to negative input.

Good Reports

What should we do when we know or hear something negative about a Christian brother or sister? Do we share it? Squelch it? Stew over it? Pray about it? How do we effectively handle the hot potato of negative news?

Our natural response to an offense in someone else's life is to use it for slander, gossip, murmuring, or beguilement. This results not in the restoration of the offender, but rather in his alienation. It's not long until he feels that everyone is against him. This then plants seeds of resentment and bitterness in his heart which drive a wedge between him and his fellow believers. Occasionally, some will sense he is being mistreated and rally to his cause. This results in choosing up sides and waging a divisive war in the fellowship of God's people.

Jesus Christ clearly instructs how to respond to one who has sinned. Implementing this process productively protects our newfound joy of a tongue in check. Five steps of success in responding to negative information are found in Matthew 18:15-17.

1. *Recognize our "familyship"* (Matt. 18:15). At a family gathering one of my nieces blurted out, "Daddy, isn't this good familyship?" She was aware of the fact that there was a special bond between family members. As Christians, we have a special oneness in Christ. Our unity calls for living, protecting, supporting, and helping one another. When a Christian brother or sister sins, we are to respond in family love. Our bond in Christ needs to be an undeniable reality that prompts us to love one another. It's a matter of familyship.

In this context, it is significant that Christ said, "If your *brother* sins against you." When your brothers or sisters in Christ sin, what is your first response? Is it to nail them to the wall behind their backs, or is it to attempt to heal, support, protect, and love? If there is anything to our Christianity, then it must be the latter (John 13:34-35). If we are unwilling to accept our family responsibilities one to another, then we will verbally destroy each other.

2. *Have a clear perception of the problem* (Matt. 18:15). We must be sure that the other person has indeed sinned. If it is not clear-cut that our brother has actually sinned, we

should ask ourselves several questions: *Am I being overly sensitive? Are sufficient facts in? Is this first, second, third, or twenty-third-hand information? Does this offense actually violate scriptural teaching or does it violate certain expectations and preferences? Am I responding negatively because of a past offense?*

With these questions in mind, our hearts are open to a greater understanding of the situation as we follow step three. No final conclusions should be drawn until step three has been taken.

3. *Demonstrate God's love* (Matt. 18:15). This step has three important dynamics:

A. *Go to him.* Because God loved us, He took the initiative to come to us (Gen. 3; John 3:16). It is crucial that we be willing to approach those who have sinned against us with the intent of restoring them. Timing is important to keep in mind as we make this approach. Praying that God will provide the right opportunity is an important prelude.

Galatians 6:1 gives some important instructions for our attitudes in approaching a brother who has sinned. We must be spiritual—in tune and in fellowship with God; gentle—without bitterness, revenge, or hostility in our hearts, willing to see the problem from his point of view; and cautious—taking care lest, in the process, we too fall into sin (anger, bitterness, sins of the tongue).

B. *Show him his fault.* This must be done lovingly and carefully. It is important that we convey love through our attitudes and words; avoid a judgmental, "holier than thou" attitude; and listen carefully with an open mind to the facts, his point of view, and his attitude (defensive, hostile, repentant, proud, etc.)

C. *Just between the two of you.* It is of utmost importance that these matters be shared first between you and the offender. In fact, it produces great freedom in the interchange if you can assure the one you are talking to that you have discussed this with no one!

If our brother responds, he is restored to God's fellowship and to ours. The information should then be dropped and separated "as far as the east is from the west" (Ps. 103:12). If, however, he does not respond positively, and if the offense is of such a nature as to pursue the matter, we need to be committed to Christ's next command.

4. *Demonstrate God's love with one or two others* (Matt. 18:16). This commitment pursues the matter of loving restoration. We should choose carefully those who return with us. They should be people who won't take sides. They should also be people whom our offender respects. They should share our goal of loving restoration and our commitment to the three attitudes of Galatians 6:1. They should have clean consciences with the offender. It would also be helpful if these companions have been through the same problem as the offender so that they can counsel from experience and assure him of potential victory.

The purpose of this commitment is to restore the offender and establish the truth of the situation in the mouths of two or three witnesses. At this point, if the offender refuses to respond to the love of his brothers, if necessary the matter should be taken to the church.

5. *Demonstrate God's love through the church* (Matt. 18:17). Along with the individuals who confronted the offender with you, you should approach the constituted church leadership (pastor or official board) and lovingly share the sin problem that you have been attempting to restore. The church leadership should then, under their constituted procedure, approach the offender in the same frame of reference as the earlier steps. If the offender does not respond to this attempt at restoration, then he is to be released from the fellowship of the church and treated as a "heathen and as a tax collector" (v. 17).

All general conversation then is to be filled with good reports about one another. Bad news should be limited to just the few who play a part in the solution and the restoration of the brother in question. When we fill our conversation with good reports of one another, it produces gratefulness toward each other, a spirit of joy, and a stimulation to grow in the Lord.

A commitment to bearing only good reports does have some exceptions in Scripture. God's Word states that in our relationship to our husbands and wives, we are as one. Though there may be times when we don't wish to burden our partners with negative information, when it is appropriate their counsel and prayer support will prove to be a valuable resource. Both husband and wife must share the commitments of confidentiality and a Spirit-controlled tongue.

At times, some situations will require special insight and perspective. The need for godly advice may become necessary. God's Word reminds us that there is wisdom in a multitude of counselors (Prov. 11:14). But we should seek counsel carefully. Choosing a neutral counselor who does not know the situation or the people involved preserves the anonymity of those involved and protects their reputations.

In the New Testament, church leaders at times warned the flock about false teachers and individuals who would hurt the assembly if they were not exposed. When this becomes necessary, it should be done as it was in Scripture; specific details of the sin are not shared, and it is done with tears (1 Tim. 1:18-20; Phil. 3:18-19).

Constructive Responses

How do we respond to those who violate our biblical commitments in conversation with us? "The heart of the righteous studieth [how] to answer; but the mouth of the wicked poureth out evil things" (Prov. 15:28, KJV). Our answers to those who sin with their tongues in front of us are crucial to the continuation of our new-found joy and in the restoration of those speaking to us.

As we think back through our commitments, we see seven ways in which we can wisely respond:

1. *Do not communicate approval of what is being said or encourage additional statements about the matter* (1 Thes. 5:15, 22; 1 Tim. 5:22). Approval and encouragement can be communicated both verbally and physically. When being talked to, many times we nod our heads to show that we are listening. However, a nod of the head will often be interpreted as agreement and will encourage the sin to continue. Even if what the person shares is true, we must not give the impression that we are condoning his violation of a biblical principle. It is better to quietly listen with no visual, verbal, or physical response until we have the first opportunity to interject a change in the course of the conversation.

2. *Pray for wisdom* (James 1:5-7). While you are listening, send up a quick prayer for wisdom. By the time the encounter is finished, you will be surprised how God has helped you.

3. *Respond in the context of your own commitments.* Honestly respond by encouraging submission to God's perspective in the matter and by reflecting a submission to the well-being of the one spoken about. By patiently hesitating, evaluating, and resisting the sins of anger you will help turn the focus to God and a loving resolution. Maintain love by encouraging the one who shares the information to look for ways to meet the needs of the offender. And keep your personal commitment to good reports in mind.

4. *Avoid a judgmental spirit* (Gal. 5:22; 6:1). Be sure to communicate love in any statement you make. A judgmental or rude spirit will only alienate and make it impossible to lead the one you are speaking with to the joy of a Spirit-controlled tongue.

5. *Encourage them to control their tongues.* When someone is about to tell you a juicy tidbit, you have the option of saying, "Tell me about the details," or encouraging them not to violate God's principles. A short statement like, "Don't tell me; I already have more negative thoughts than I know what to do with" should stop the bad news before it gets started.

Many times at social gatherings someone will get just far enough into a story to have everyone's attention and then say, "You know, I really shouldn't say this," to which we all respond, "Oh, come on—you can't stop now! We won't tell." It would be refreshing to hear someone say, "Good for you. Don't tell. I admire your self-control."

6. *Pray about what you hear* (Phil. 4:6-7; 1 Peter 5:7). Pray for healing, conviction, growth, reconciliation, wisdom, or whatever is appropriate. As you pray, God will direct your responses.

7. *Publicly share your commitment to a Spirit-controlled tongue.* As others become aware of your personal desire to have a controlled tongue, they will become sensitive not to share wrong information with you. The best way to avoid the embarrassment of being party to an uncontrolled tongue is to control *your* tongue and let others know of your commitment. Tactfully share your commitment with your family, friends, and church. Ask them to patiently encourage and pray for you.

Nurturing our inner maturity, restricting our conversation to good reports, and being constructive in the face of negative input will not only fortify and stimulate our growth, but it will infect others with an awareness of the positive benefit of a tongue in check!

Words fitly spoken are like apples of gold in pictures of silver—a tree of life to all who hear (Prov. 25:11; 15:4). They are the Lord's delight!